need to know?

Speak
Spanish

Collins

First published in 2005 by Collins
an imprint of
HarperCollins Publishers
Westerhill Road, Bishopbriggs
Glasgow G64 2QT

www.collins.co.uk

A catalogue record for this book is available from
the British Library

Editor: Caroline Smart
Text: Harry Campbell
Spanish Consultants: Lydia Batanaz Arteaga,
Cordelia Lilly, Sue Tyson-Ward
Other contributors: Henrietta T. Brunton
Series design: Mark Thomson
Front cover photograph: Emile D'Edesse
© Impact Photos

isbn 0 00 719330 0

Typeset by Davidson Pre-Press Graphics Ltd,
Glasgow
Printed and bound by Scotprint, Haddington

Contents

◎ **Reference Zone**

Introduction

Are you one of those people who want to learn Spanish, but have never quite managed? Perhaps, after numerous attempts, you still don't feel on top of the basics. *Collins Speak Spanish* is for you! This course is designed for those with some knowledge of Spanish, but who would like to learn more, or be shown that they do indeed know more than they think.

We do this through a series of dialogues. You can listen to the dialogues on CD1 and then explore the conversations in more depth in the book. The dialogues provide a snapshot of Spanish while the points highlighted in each unit reveal how the language works – sometimes in a logical way, but often not!

We pick out of each unit the most important vocabulary, and then add a number of extra words to learn, often on a slightly different theme. Then it's your chance to speak Spanish in the short exercises at the end of each unit.

The second part of the book, which relates to CD2, gives you the nitty-gritty – all the practical stuff that goes into a language – numbers, time, nouns, verbs and so on. Each section is tracked so you can decide what to focus on and there are lots of examples showing how Spanish works. *Collins Speak Spanish* is a basic introduction to the language. If you want all the detail, we recommend the *Collins Easy Learning* range: *Spanish Grammar*, *Spanish Verbs* and *Spanish Dictionary*.

So that you don't have to rely on listening to the CDs to get the pronunciation right, the book features an easy-to-follow pronunciation system. This means the book and CDs can be used independently. For a full explanation of how to use this course, turn to the *How to use* section on p14.

We hope that this original approach to language learning is one that works for you, and gives you the confidence to go on and speak Spanish. You may even enjoy it!

Points about English

Mary **works in a small** shop. **She sells** cheese, fruit **and** vegetables. **She usually gets up early in the morning because** the shop **opens at 8 o'clock. She lives in** the centre **of Manchester.**

verbs

These are the words that tell you the action of the sentence: **works**, **sells**. In English you use words like I, she or they (pronouns), with the verb to show who is doing the action: I **go**, you **go**, he **goes**, we **go**, etc. When it's not specified who is performing the action, you sometimes find the word 'to' in front of it: to work, to sell, to be. This is known as the 'infinitive'; you could think of it as the starting point for an 'infinite' number of ways that the verb can go.

nouns and articles

Nouns are labels for anything you can give a name to: **market**, **cheese**, **house**. A noun doesn't have to be a solid thing; it can be something abstract like **morning**, or it can be the name of something specific like a person or place: **Mary**, **Manchester** (such nouns, spelt with a capital letter, are called 'proper' nouns). When there is more than one of something, the 'plural' form is used; in English, this most often involves adding an -s (**markets**, **mornings**) though many words have irregular plurals (**man/men**, **sheep/sheep**). In English the definitive article is **the** and **a** or **some**.

adjectives

Adjectives are words that describe a thing or person, to give extra information about them: a **small** market, a **tall** girl, **young** Mary, the work is **enjoyable**, Manchester is **big**. In English the adjective generally goes in front of the noun, and it's the same whatever the word it describes: **pretty** girl, **pretty** girls, a **slim** girl, a **slim** boy.

adverbs

An adverb is a word that describes a verb or an adjective – how, when or where something is done: Mary gets up **early**, she drives **carefully** and works **quickly**. Often, though not always, English adverbs are made by adding -ly to an adjective: **careful/carefully**; **quick/quickly**. But many of the most common adverbs are irregular: **early**, **fast**, **well**. Examples of adverbs applying to adjectives are **very early**, **incredibly pretty**, **very good**.

prepositions

Prepositions usually indicate a relationship such as position or time: **in** a small market, **near** the centre of Manchester, **at** 8 o'clock. Sometimes one language uses a preposition where it is not needed in the other, just as you can say either 'I wrote to my mother' or (in American English) 'I wrote my mother'.

Points about Spanish

Mary trabaja en un pequeño negocio. Vende queso, fruto y verduras. Se levanta temprano porque el negocio abre a las ocho. Vive en una casa en el centro de Manchester.

verbs

In Spanish the infinitive is just one word, such as **andar** 'to walk', and there are various different endings according to who is 'doing' the action: **andas** 'you walk', **andamos** 'we walk', **andan** 'they walk' and so on, where English usually has just two, 'walk' and 'walks'. Spanish verbs divide into three main sorts, according to the infinitive ending: **-ar (andar)**, **-er (comer**, 'to eat') or **-ir (vivir**, 'to live'). But some of the most common verbs are irregular, just as in English we normally say 'I am', 'you are' and 'he is' rather than 'I be', 'you be' and 'he bes'!

nouns and articles

All Spanish nouns are either 'masculine' or 'feminine'. These are just terms used to describe the way a word behaves grammatically: it doesn't mean that the thing itself necessarily has male or female characteristics. Generally speaking nouns ending in **-o** are masculine, and those ending in **-a** feminine. Adding **-s** or **-es** is the standard way to make a plural in Spanish. The 'articles', **el/los** and **la/las** 'the', and **un/unos** and **una/unas** 'a', 'some' tell you the gender: **el café** 'the coffee' (masculine), **las tazas** (feminine) 'the cups'.

adverbs

In Spanish most adverbs are made by adding **-mente** to the adjective in its feminine form: **rapido** 'quick' **rapidamente** 'quickly'. But many of the most common ones are irregular: **bien** 'well', **pronto** 'soon', **temprano** 'early'.

prepositions

These work much as in English – **en** 'in', 'on', 'at', **de** 'from', 'of', and so on – except that sometimes Spanish may not use the preposition you'd expect. For example, while English speakers 'depend on something', Spanish speakers '**dependen de**' it.

adjectives

In Spanish, adjectives usually 'agree' with the noun they describe. If a word is masculine, the adjective stays in the basic form given in dictionaries, such as **un pequeño negocio**, but if not, the feminine ending **-a** is usually needed – **una pequeña casa**. To make adjectives plural, then **-s** or **-es** are usually added.

pronouns

To avoid repeating 'Mary', we use a pronoun, 'she', in subsequent references. In Spanish, the verb ending usually tells you who is doing the action, so the pronoun can be dropped: **vende** rather than **ella vende**.

Pronunciation guide

To make it as clear as possible how to pronounce the Spanish in the book, we've supplied a phonetic transcription (re-spelling) of each phrase. It's only intended as a rough guide, since it's not possible to represent Spanish sounds accurately using English spelling. We use hypens to break up words into syllables to help show how the stress works, and to make the transcription as clear and unambiguous as possible. Don't try to pronounce the syllables separately though, just run them together naturally as you would when speaking your own language.

Spanish pronunciation isn't difficult, and unlike English has the advantage of being predictable and logical. Once you learn a few basic rules, it shouldn't be too long before you can read straight from the Spanish without bothering with the transcription.

The vowels are very straightforward. There are five, and each has just one sound, unlike in English ('sat', 'safe', 'sofa' etc). The sound is always 'pure', meaning it does not start in one position and move to another like the standard English pronunciation of 'o' 'rope' or 'a' 'tape'. So **a** is something like the one in 'tap', never 'tape'; **e** is always as in 'pet', never 'peat'; **i** is always 'ee' as in 'meet'; **o** is something like 'hop', never 'hope'; **u** is always 'oo' as in 'hoop', rather than the English sound of 'hut'.

Where two vowels come together, unless one of them has an accent on it, they are run together to form a single syllable. However, they keep their sound even in combination with other letters, so **au** (**autobús** *aoo-tob-**oos***) is 'a' plus 'oo', like English 'ow', not like the 'aw' sound of English 'automatic'. We've shown that in the pronunciation as *aoo*. Likewise **eu** as in **euros** is not the English sound of 'you' or 'yer', but 'e' followed by 'oo': *eoo*. So the individual letters maintain their value when run together with others.

Most consonant letters are pronounced as in English: **b**, **ch**, **d**, **f**, **k**, **l**, **m**, **n**, **p**, **s**, **t**, **y** and (usually) **w** and **x**. The exceptions are shown below:

Spanish	sounds a bit like	example	transcription
c	c_at	comer	ko-**mer**
c (before e/i)	think	cinco	**theenk**-o
g	g_ot	gafas	**ga**-fass
g (before e/i)	loch	general	khen-er-**al**
z	think	zapatos	tha-**pa**-toss
j	loch	hijo	**eekh**-o
qu	kick (*not* 'quick')	quiero	**kyer**-o
ll	million	calle	**kal**-yay or **ka**-yay
ñ	onion	mañana	man-**ya**-na

The letter **h** is always silent, **qu** is like English 'k', not 'kw', and **s** is always a hissing *ss*, not a voiced z. The single and double **r** / **rr** are traditionally considered separate letters in Spanish, and are pronounced differently; **rr** is rolled strongly, while **r** is just a quick tap of the tongue.

Some consonants are affected by the vowel following them. The letter **c** before the 'weak' or 'soft' vowels **e** or **i**, is pronounced like 'th' in 'thin', as is the letter **z** in any position. Likewise the letter **g** before **e** or **i** has the rasping sound found in the Scottish word 'loch', which we show as *kh*; and **j** always has this sound.

Spanish **b** and **v** are pronounced exactly the same, like a loose version of English 'b', and the pronunciation of **d** and **g** also tends to be much less 'hard' and crisp than in English. In most cases the **d** blurs into the voiced 'th' sound of 'this' (not the invoiced one of 'think'), while the **g** is like a very loose pronunciation of 'mugger' – make an effort to enunciate less! Sometimes these sounds more or less disappear altogether, so **agua** can be ***a**-wa*, and **Madrid** *mad-**ree***.

The **ll** is traditionally pronounced as a combination of **l** and **y**, a bit like the 'lli' of English million run together as one sound. However it more often than not comes out as a simple **y** sound: ***ko**-mo say **yam**-a* instead of ***ko**-mo say **lyam**-a* for ¿cómo se llama?

Spanish, like English, places more stress (emphasis) on some parts of the word than others, which is what makes the difference between **por qué** 'why?' and **porque** 'because', or in English 'an <u>ex</u>port' and 'to ex<u>port</u>'. The syllable to be stressed is shown in the transcription in ***bold*** type: **porque** ***por**-kay*.

Often a stressed syllable has an accent, which in Spanish is always the 'acute' sort (´). But generally an accent is only necessary if the word does not fit the default stress pattern, where the stress comes either on the last syllable, or, in cases where the word ends in a vowel or the letters **n** or **s**, the next-to-last syllable. So, **comer** and **verdad** (stressed on the last syllable), and **casa**, **madre** and **lunes** (stressed on next-to-last syllable) do not need an accent, but **estación**, **cuídate** and **miércoles** do. Note that two vowels together count as one syllable if one of them is weak (**i** or **u**), just as English 'you' and 'we' are one syllable even though they consist of two vowels together (*ee**oo*** and *oo**ee***).

However there is another reason for adding an accent to a word, even if it's not needed for pronunciation purposes, and that is to distinguish two basic words that would otherwise look the same, such as **si** 'if' and **sí** 'yes', or **tu** 'your' and **tú** 'you'. Words like **donde** 'where', **como** 'how' and **quien** 'who' have an accent when they are a question, but not when stringing together two smaller phrases into a sentence. Contrast ¿**cuándo llegas?** 'when do you arrive?' and **cuando llegas** 'when you arrive', or ¿**sabes qué hace?** 'do you know <u>what</u> he's doing?' and ¿**sabes que es inglés?** 'do you know <u>that</u> he's English?'

useful websites

> **BBC resources for learning Spanish**
  http://www.bbc.co.uk/languages/spanish/
> **WordReference.com**
  http://www.wordreference.com/index.htm
> **About.com: vocabulary, proverbs, dictionaries, links, etc**
  http://spanish.about.com
> **Dictionary of Spanish with audio files**
  http://www.spanishdict.com
> **lessons, vocabulary builder, verb conjugator, exercises**
  http://www.donquijote.org/

Dialogue Zone

The dialogues provide a snapshot of Spanish, while the points highlighted show how the language works. We pick out of each dialogue the most useful vocabulary and then add a number of extra words to learn, often on a slightly different theme. Then its your chance to speak Spanish in the short exercise on the following track.

How to use *Speak Spanish*

The book comes with two CDs. Purple CD1, the Dialogue Zone, contains the dialogues, vocabulary and practice. Blue CD2, the Reference Zone, contains the nuts and bolts: numbers, days, months, etc. It goes with the final section of the book.

purple CD1 track number

Dialogue Zone

There are 16 dialogues. Each one begins with an even track number: 2 is 'At the tourist office', 4 is 'A chance encounter' and so on. The practice sessions following each conversation begin with an odd number: 3, 5, 7, etc.

Try listening to the dialogues first, without referring to the book, to see how much you understand.

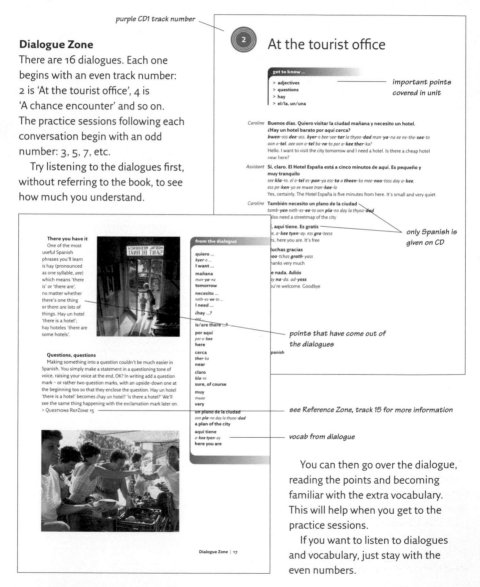

At the tourist office

important points covered in unit

get to know ...
> adjectives
> questions
> hay
> el/la, un/una

Caroline Buenos días. Quiero visitar la ciudad mañana y necesito un hotel. ¿Hay un hotel barato por aquí cerca?
bwen-oss dee-*ass*. kyer-o bee-see-*tar* la thyoo-*dad* man-*ya*-na ee ne-the-*see*-to oon o-*tel*. aee oon o-*tel* ba-*ra*-to por a-*kee ther*-ka?
Hello. I want to visit the city tomorrow and I need a hotel. Is there a cheap hotel near here?

Assistant Sí, claro. El Hotel España está a cinco minutos de aquí. Es pequeño y muy tranquilo
see *kla*-ro. el o-*tel* es-*pan*-ya ess-*ta* a *theen*-ko mee-*noo*-toss day a-*kee*. ess pe-*ken*-yo ee mwee tran-*kee*-lo
Yes, certainly. The Hotel España is five minutes from here. It's small and very quiet

Caroline También necesito un plano de la ciudad
tamb-*yen* neth-es-*ee*-to oon *pla*-no day la thyoo-*dad*
Also need a streetmap of the city

..., aquí tiene. Es gratis
..e, a-*kee tyen*-ay. ess *gra*-teess
..es, here you are. It's free

only Spanish is given on CD

..uchas gracias
..oo-tchas *grath*-yass
..anks very much

..e nada. Adiós
..y na-da. ad-*yoss*
..u're welcome. Goodbye

There you have it
One of the most useful Spanish phrases you'll learn is hay (pronounced as one syllable, *aee*) which means 'there is' or 'there are', no matter whether there's one thing or there are lots of things. Hay un hotel 'there is a hotel'; hay hoteles 'there are some hotels'.

Questions, questions
Making something into a question couldn't be much easier in Spanish. You simply make a statement in a questioning tone of voice, raising your voice at the end, OK? In writing add a question mark – or rather two question marks, with an upside-down one at the beginning too so that they enclose the question. Hay un hotel 'there is a hotel' becomes ¿hay un hotel? 'is there a hotel?' We'll see the same thing happening with the exclamation mark later on.
> QUESTIONS RefZONE 15

from the dialogue

quiero ...
kyer-o ...
I want ...

mañana
man-*ya*-na
tomorrow

necesito ...
neth-es-*ee*-to ...
I need ...

¿hay ...?
aee ...
is/are there ...?

por aquí
por a-*kee*
here

cerca
ther-ka
near

claro
kla-ro
sure, of course

muy
mwee
very

un plano de la ciudad
oon *pla*-no day la thyoo-*dad*
a plan of the city

aquí tiene
a-*kee tyen*-ay
here you are

points that have come out of the dialogues

see Reference Zone, track 15 for more information

vocab from dialogue

You can then go over the dialogue, reading the points and becoming familiar with the extra vocabulary. This will help when you get to the practice sessions.

If you want to listen to dialogues and vocabulary, just stay with the even numbers.

Dialogue Zone | 17

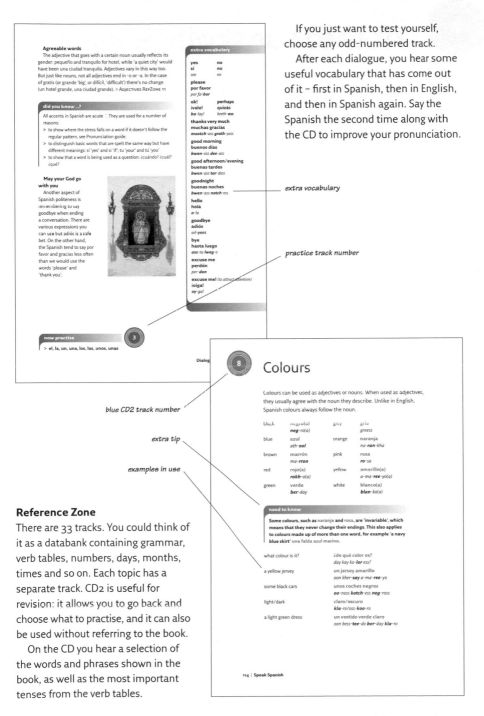

If you just want to test yourself, choose any odd-numbered track.

After each dialogue, you hear some useful vocabulary that has come out of it – first in Spanish, then in English, and then in Spanish again. Say the Spanish the second time along with the CD to improve your pronunciation.

Agreeable words
The adjective that goes with a certain noun usually reflects its gender: pequeño and tranquilo for hotel, while 'a quiet city' would have been una ciudad tranquila. Adjectives vary in this way too. But just like nouns, not all adjectives end in -o or -a. In the case of gratis (or grande 'big', or difícil, 'difficult') there's no change (un hotel grande, una ciudad grande). > Adjectives RefZone 11

did you know ...?
All accents in Spanish are acute ´. They are used for a number of reasons:
> to show where the stress falls on a word if it doesn't follow the regular pattern, see Pronunciation guide.
> to distinguish basic words that are spelt the same way but have different meanings: sí 'yes' and si 'if'; tu 'your' and tú 'you'
> to show that a word is being used as a question: ¿cuándo? ¿cuál? ¿qué?

May your God go with you
Another aspect of Spanish politeness is remembering to say goodbye when ending a conversation. There are various expressions you can use but adiós is a safe bet. On the other hand, the Spanish tend to say por favor and gracias less often than we would use the words 'please' and 'thank you'.

extra vocabulary

yes	no
sí	no
see	*no*
please	
por favor	
por fa-bor	
ok!	perhaps
¡vale!	quizás
ba-lay!	*keeth-ass*
thanks very much	
muchas gracias	
mootch-ass grath-yass	
good morning	
buenos días	
bwen-oss dee-ass	
good afternoon/evening	
buenas tardes	
bwen-ass tar-dess	
goodnight	
buenas noches	
bwen-ass notch-ess	
hello	
hola	
o-la	
goodbye	
adiós	
ad-yass	
bye	
hasta luego	
ass-ta lweg-o	
excuse me	
perdón	
per-don	
excuse me! *(to attract attention)*	
¡oiga!	
oy-ga!	

extra vocabulary

practice track number

now practise 3
> el, la, un, una, los, las, unos, unas

blue CD2 track number

extra tip

examples in use

Reference Zone

There are 33 tracks. You could think of it as a databank containing grammar, verb tables, numbers, days, months, times and so on. Each topic has a separate track. CD2 is useful for revision: it allows you to go back and choose what to practise, and it can also be used without referring to the book.

On the CD you hear a selection of the words and phrases shown in the book, as well as the most important tenses from the verb tables.

8 # Colours

Colours can be used as adjectives or nouns. When used as adjectives, they usually agree with the noun they describe. Unlike in English, Spanish colours always follow the noun.

black	negro(a) **neg**-ro(a)	grey	gris greess
blue	azul ath-**ool**	orange	naranja na-**ran**-kha
brown	marrón ma-**rron**	pink	rosa **ro**-sa
red	rojo(a) **rokh**-o(a)	yellow	amarillo(a) a-ma-**ree**-yo(a)
green	verde **ber**-day	white	blanco(a) **blan**-ko(a)

need to know
Some colours, such as naranja and rosa, are 'invariable', which means that they never change their endings. This also applies to colours made up of more than one word, for example 'a navy blue skirt' una falda azul marino.

what colour is it?	¿de qué color es? *day kay ko-lor ess?*
a yellow jersey	un jersey amarillo *oon kher-say a-ma-ree-yo*
some black cars	unos coches negros *oo-noss kotch-ess neg-ross*
light/dark	claro/oscuro *kla-ro/oss-koo-ro*
a light green dress	un vestido verde claro *oon bess-tee-do ber-day kla-ro*

114 | Speak Spanish

At the tourist office

get to know …

> adjectives
> questions
> hay
> el/la, un/una

Caroline **Buenos días. Quiero visitar la ciudad mañana y necesito un hotel. ¿Hay un hotel barato por aquí cerca?**
*bwen-oss **dee**-ass. **kyer**-o bee-see-**tar** la thyoo-**dad** man-**ya**-na ee ne-the-**see**-to oon o-**tel**. aee oon o-**tel** ba-**ra**-to por a-**kee ther**-ka?*
Hello. I want to visit the city tomorrow and I need a hotel. Is there a cheap hotel near here?

Assistant **Sí, claro. El Hotel España está a cinco minutos de aquí. Es pequeño y muy tranquilo**
*see **kla**-ro. el o-**tel** es-**pan**-ya ess-**ta** a **theen**-ko mee-**noo**-toss day a-**kee**. ess pe-**ken**-yo ee mwee tran-**kee**-lo*
Yes, certainly. The Hotel España is five minutes from here. It's small and very quiet

Caroline **También necesito un plano de la ciudad**
*tamb-**yen** neth-es-**ee**-to oon **pla**-no day la thyoo-**dad***
I also need a streetmap of the city

Assistant **Sí, aquí tiene. Es gratis**
*see, a-**kee tyen**-ay. ess **gra**-teess*
Yes, here you are. It's free

Caroline **Muchas gracias**
***moo**-tchas **grath**-yass*
Thanks very much

Assistant **De nada. Adiós**
*day **na**-da. ad-**yoss***
You're welcome. Goodbye

There you have it

One of the most useful Spanish phrases you'll learn is hay (pronounced as one syllable, *aee*) which means 'there is' or 'there are', no matter whether there's one thing or there are lots of things. Hay un hotel 'there is a hotel'; hay hoteles 'there are some hotels'.

Questions, questions

Making something into a question couldn't be much easier in Spanish. You simply make a statement in a questioning tone of voice, raising your voice at the end, OK? In writing add a question mark – or rather two question marks, with an upside-down one at the beginning too so that they enclose the question. Hay un hotel 'there is a hotel' becomes ¿hay un hotel? 'is there a hotel?' We'll see the same thing happening with the exclamation mark later on.

> QUESTIONS REFZONE 15

> QUESTIONS REFZONE 15

from the dialogue

quiero ...
kyer-o ...
I want ...

mañana
man-ya-na
tomorrow

necesito ...
neth-es-ee-to ...
I need ...

¿hay ...?
aee ...?
is/are there ...?

por aquí
por a-kee
here

cerca
ther-ka
near

claro
kla-ro
sure, of course

muy
mwee
very

aquí tiene
a-kee tyen-ay
here you are

Pink or blue

In Spanish the words for 'the' and 'a' vary depending on whether the word referred to is masculine or feminine, and singular or plural. It's el and un before a masculine singular noun, and la and una before a feminine singular noun. As hotel is masculine in Spanish, 'the hotel' is el hotel and 'a hotel' is un hotel. On the other hand ciudad is feminine, so 'the city' is la ciudad and 'a city' is una ciudad. We'll look at the plural forms later.

It's a boy!

Why should hotels be boys and cities be girls, you may wonder? Well, they just are. In most cases the clue is in the ending: -o for masculine words and -a for feminine ones – but we're out of luck here. You just have to know that hotel is masculine and ciudad, like other words ending in -dad, is feminine.
> Nouns & Articles RefZone 10

Thanks for nothing

When someone says thank you, it's polite to reply de nada, literally 'for nothing', or no hay de qué 'there is no need'. It's equivalent to 'you're welcome' or 'not at all'.

Clear as mud

You will often hear the word claro in Spanish. It's often translated as 'of course' but it's probably closer to the American use of 'sure'. Sometimes it really just means 'yes'.

Agreeable words

The adjective that goes with a certain noun usually reflects its gender: pequeño and tranquilo for hotel, while 'a quiet city' would have been una ciudad tranquila. Adjectives vary in this way too. But just like nouns, not all adjectives end in -o or -a. In the case of gratis (or grande 'big', or difícil, 'difficult') there's no change (un hotel grande, una ciudad grande). > ADJECTIVES REFZONE 11

> ADJECTIVES REFZONE 11

did you know ...?

All accents in Spanish are acute ´. They are used for a number of reasons:

> to show where the stress falls on a word if it doesn't follow the regular pattern, see Pronunciation guide.

> to distinguish basic words that are spelt the same way but have different meanings: sí 'yes' and si 'if'; tu 'your' and tú 'you'

> to show that a word is being used as a question: ¿cuándo? ¿cuál? ¿qué?

May your God go with you

Another aspect of Spanish politeness is remembering to say goodbye when ending a conversation. There are various expressions you can use but adiós is a safe bet. On the other hand, the Spanish tend to say por favor and gracias less often than we would use the words 'please' and 'thank you'.

now practise

> **el, la, un, una, los, las, unos, unas**

A chance encounter

get to know ...

> **formal usted**
> **estar**
> **unos/unas**
> **saying goodbyes**

Ana **Buenos días María, ¿cómo está?**
*bwen-oss **dee**-ass ma-**ree**-a, **ko**-mo ess-**ta**?*
Good morning María, how are you?

María **Bien, gracias, ¿y usted?**
*byen, **grath**-yass, ee oo-**sted**?*
Fine, thanks, and you?

Ana **Muy bien. ¿Qué tal está su marido?**
*mwee byen. kay tal ess-**ta** soo ma-**ree**-do?*
Very well. How's your husband?

María **Está muy bien, gracias. ¿Cómo están los nietos?**
*ess-**ta** mwee byen, **grath**-yass. **ko**-mo ess-**tan** los **nyet**-oss?*
He's fine, thanks. How are the grandchildren?

Ana **Bien. Están en el colegio. Bueno, tengo que hacer unas compras**
*byen. ess-**tan** en el ko-**lekh**-yo. **bwen**-o, **ten**-go kay ath-**er oo**-nass **kom**-prass*
Fine. They're at school. Well, I have to do some shopping

María **Hasta luego. Cuídese**
*ass-ta **lweg**-o. **kwee**-day-say*
See you later. Take care

Ana **Igualmente. Adiós**
*eeg-wal-**men**-tay. ad-**yoss***
You too. Goodbye

¿cómo está?
ko-mo ess-ta?
how are you?

bien
byen
well

gracias
***grath**-yass*
thanks

¿qué tal está ...?
*kay tal ess-**ta** ...?*
how is ...?

su marido
*soo ma-**ree**-do*
your husband

en el colegio
*el ko-**lekh**-yo*
at school

tengo que ...
***ten**-go kay ...*
I have to ...

hacer unas compras
*ath-**er** oo-nass **kom**-prass*
to do some shopping

igualmente
*eeg-wal-**men**-tay*
same to you/you too

To be or not to be?

Notice how often the word está or están crops up in this passage. It's from the verb estar, the verb 'to be' – or at least one of the verbs for 'to be'. As we'll see later, Spanish has two ways of saying 'to be', depending on the circumstances. This is the one you use for asking what state someone or something is in, in other words how they are at the moment, as opposed to what they are like normally. You may be puzzled to see both verbs in el Hotel España está a cinco minutos de aquí ... es pequeño y muy tranquilo. This is because when giving the position or location of something, even immovable objects like buildings or cities, you use estar. Don't worry, we'll be returning to this topic ...

Pronouns away!

In phrases like ¿cómo está? 'how are you?' and están en el colegio 'they are at school' you'll notice there is no single word (pronoun) to represent the person involved ('you' and 'they' in this case). You could have said ¿cómo está usted? and ellos están en el colegio but it's normal to drop the pronoun most of the time, unless it's really needed to avoid ambiguity. But since Spanish has different verb endings to make it clear who is doing or being what, it can do without the pronoun most of the time. For example, estoy bien 'I'm fine' but estamos bien 'we're fine'. So it's important to learn your verb endings!

Why so formal?

In Spanish there is more than one word for 'you'. Among people who know each other only slightly, especially older people, or in formal contexts, the word usted is often used. This word, sometimes abbreviated in writing to Vd or Ud, comes from an old expression literally meaning 'your honour'. So grammatically it takes the endings that go with he/she/it, because strictly speaking you are asking 'how *is* your honour' rather than 'how *are* you?' So we see the same form of the verb, está (from estar) used for 'how are *you*?' in ¿cómo está? and 'how is *he* (your husband)?' in ¿qué tal está su marido? You might think this would cause confusion, but in practice the context makes things clear, and if not you can always specify using the relevant word, such as usted 'you', él 'he' or ella 'she'.

Boys rule OK!

We've already seen that there is more than one word in Spanish for 'the'. In fact, there are four, depending on whether the word is masculine or feminine, singular or plural. We've seen el and la for the singular, and los for the masculine plural. The feminine plural is las. And if you're referring to a mixed-sex group of people or things, males take priority – it's los. For all we know, Ana's nietos (grandchildren) may include some nietas (granddaughters).

What cheer?

One of the most useful basic expressions in Spanish is ¿qué tal? 'how's things?', 'how is/was it?', 'any joy?' etc. You can use it to ask how someone is, what something is like, how something went, whatever. You can also follow it up with the name of a person or thing, for example in ¿qué tal su marido?, which is similar to ¿cómo está su marido? 'how is your husband?', except that there's no verb in there to change in the plural ¿cómo están los nietos? 'how are the grandchildren?' So it's a bit vaguer 'how's it going with your husband, what news of your husband?', and easier to use.

Begging the question

When someone asks you a question and you want to ask them the same thing back, you simply use the word y 'and' followed by the relevant word for 'you'. So here we have ¿cómo está? – bien, y usted? 'how are you? fine, and you?'

One + one = some

We know un and una mean 'a' for singular nouns. They can also be translated as 'one'. In unas compras 'some shopping (purchases)' we have the plural equivalent, unas (or unos for masculine plural), which is equivalent to English 'some'.

Hasta la vista, baby

Yes, Arnie's catchphrase is actually proper Spanish – give or take the word 'baby' of course. The word hasta means 'until' (so hasta luego is literally 'until later', ie 'see you later') and you can use it to form an unlimited number of farewells, just as we use 'see you ...' in English: hasta lunes 'see you on Monday', hasta pronto 'see you soon', hasta otro día 'see you another day', see you again'. So hasta la vista is really 'see you next time I see you', or 'until we see each other again'.

Same to you!

To return someone's good wishes, you can simply say igualmente, which is literally 'equally, the same', in other words 'you too!' Note that typical adverb ending -mente. A regular Spanish adverb is formed by adding this ending to the adjective, in this case igual (equal). You could see it as the equivalent of the English adverb ending '-ly'.

now practise

> **saying hello and goodbye**

extra vocabulary

my family
mi familia
*mee fa-**mee**-ya*

his wife
su mujer
*soo moo-**kher***

your children
tus/sus/vuestros hijos
*tooss/sooss/**bwess**-tross **eekh**-oss*

their son
su hijo
*soo **eekh**-o*

her daughter
su hija
*soo **eekh**-a*

our parents
nuestros padres
*nwess-tross **pad**-ress*

your father
tu/su/vuestro padre
*too/soo/**bwess**-tro **pad**-ray*

my mother
mi madre
*mee **mad**-ray*

her brother
su hermano
*soo er-**ma**-no*

your sister
tu/su/vuestra hermana
*too/soo/**bwess**-tra er-**ma**-na*

Meeting an old friend

> get to know ...

> informal tú
> oye/oiga
> negatives
> contractions

Salvador **Hola Paco, ¿qué tal?**
*o-la **pa**-ko, kay tal?*
Hello Paco, how's tricks?

Paco **Muy bien, ¿y tú? Oye, ¿vamos a tomar algo?**
*mwee byen ee too? **o**-yay, **ba**-moss a tom-**ar** al-go?*
Fine, and you? Listen, shall we go and have something to drink?

Salvador **Pues no sé, estoy un poco ocupado, ¿sabes?**
*pwess no say, ess-**toy** oon **po**-ko o-koo-**pa**-do, **sa**-bess?*
Well, I don't know, I'm a bit busy, you know?

Paco **¡Venga, hombre! Invito yo**
***ben**-ga **om**-bray! een-**bee**-to yo*
Hey, come on! My treat

Salvador **Vale, está bien, pero rápido que tengo que estar pronto en casa**
***ba**-lay, ess-**ta** byen, **pe**-ro **ra**-pee-do kay **ten**-go kay ess-**tar pron**-to en **ka**-sa*
OK, all right then, but quickly because I have to be home soon

Paco **De acuerdo, vamos al bar de la esquina a tomar una cerveza**
*day a-**kwer**-do, **ba**-moss al bar day la ess-**kee**-na a tom-**ar oo**-na ther-**bay**-tha*
All right, let's go to the bar on the corner and have a beer

(later)

Salvador **Gracias por la cerveza. Me voy. Hasta otro día**
***grath**-yass por la ther-**bay**-tha. may boy, **ass**-ta **o**-tro **dee**-a*
Thanks for the beer. I'm off. See you later

Paco **De nada. Hasta luego**
*day **na**-da. **ass**-ta **lwe**-go*
No problem. See you

Among friends

The informal word for 'you', tú, is extremely widely used in Spain, especially among the young, and even between people who do not know each other particularly well. You can also make the formal/informal distinction in the plural, using ustedes and vosotros/vosotras. It's not like *tu* and *vous* in French where the plural is the same as the formal singular. Don't forget the accent on tú. It doesn't affect the pronunciation in this case, it's there to make a visual difference between two important words: without it you'd be saying not *you* but *your*.

Oy, you!

A very common way of attracting someone's attention 'excuse me!' or just a word to drop into your conversation, is oye. It comes from the verb oír 'to hear', and it's really very similar to the English use of 'listen' – or 'hey' would be another possible translation. If talking to someone you'd call usted, you say oiga instead.

That is the question

Since we only use the one question mark in English, at the end of the question, we don't have to think about where the question starts, just where it finishes. But when writing in Spanish you should remember to put your question marks around only the relevant part of the sentence: Muy bien, ¿y tú? Oye, ¿vamos a tomar algo?

Vamoose!

You might know the word vamos (also vámonos) from spaghetti Westerns – 'let's go'! It's just the 'we' form of ir 'to go', used to make a suggestion or ask a question: ¿vamos? 'shall we go?' Sí, ¡vamos! 'let's go!'

¡Everything's upside down!

Note the upside-down exclamation mark used in Spanish. As with questions, exclamation marks only go around the relevant part of the sentence (it doesn't have to be a full one).

Hey man!

Talking of spaghetti Westerns, you may be surprised that the word hombre 'man' is widely used in Spain as a sort of conversational filler, without any macho connotations, just to reinforce what you are saying. ¡Hombre, claro! Hey, obviously!

Not so

Making something negative is just as easy as making a question, ¿sabes? You put the word no before the verb: no sé 'I don't know'. There are also negative words that can be used with no such as no ... nada 'not ... anything', no ... nunca 'not ... ever'. The verb goes in the middle: no sé nada 'I don't know anything' or no como nunca 'I never eat anything'. Nada and nunca used on their own mean 'nothing' and 'never'. > Negatives RefZone 16

Getting contractions

When the word a 'to' comes up against the masculine definite article el 'the', they combine into one word al. So it's al bar 'to the bar', not a el bar. But this only affects masculine words, so a la ciudad is fine. The same thing happens when you put de 'of' or 'from' together with el. It becomes del, for example, la casa del alcalde 'the mayor's house, the house of the mayor'.

On the corner

Here we see a bar de la esquina which you might translate as 'of the corner'. However, that doesn't sound right in English. These words such as 'in', 'on', 'at', 'through' are known as prepositions and it's not always easy to know which to use. En which might appear more like 'in' can often be used to mean 'at' so en casa is 'home' or 'at home'. En el colegio is 'at' school. You'll need to learn how prepositions are used in Spanish and look up set phrases involving prepositions (such as 'to be fond of somebody', etc) in a dictionary to check the equivalent expression in Spanish.

> PREPOSITIONS REFZONE 13

> PREPOSITIONS REFZONE 13

now practise

> **negatives**

8 Making friends

get to know ...

> **ser**
> **for and since**
> **gerund (-ando)**
> **ages**

Juanjo **Hola, soy Juanjo. Tú ¿cómo te llamas?**
o-la, soy **khwan**-*kho. too* **ko**-*mo tay* **ya**-*mass?*
Hello, I'm khwan-kho. What's *your* name?

Katy **Me llamo Katy. Tengo trece años, ¿y tú?**
may **ya**-*mo* **kay**-*tee.* **ten**-*go* **treth**-*ay* **an**-*yoss, ee too?*
My name's Katy. I'm thirteen, what about you?

Juanjo **Yo tengo doce años. ¿De dónde eres?**
yo **ten**-*go* **doth**-*ay* **an**-*yoss. day* **don**-*day e-ress?*
I'm twelve. Where are you from?

Katy **Soy inglesa. Estoy de vacaciones con mis padres**
*soy een-***gless**-*a. ess-***toy** *day ba-kath-***yo**-*ness kon meess* **pa**-*dress*
I'm English. I'm on holiday with my parents

Juanjo **Yo también estoy de vacaciones, con mis padres y mi abuela. Soy de Córdoba. Tú ¿de qué ciudad eres?**
*yo tamb-***yen** *ess-***toy** *day ba-kath-***yon**-*ess, kon meess* **pa**-*dress ee mee ab-***wel**-*a.*
soy day **kor**-*do-ba. too day kay thyoo-***dad** *e-ress?*
I'm on holiday too, with my parents and my grandmother. I'm from Córdoba. Which city are *you* from?

Katy **Soy de Londres, pero ahora vivo en Gloucester. Está cerca de Bristol. Llevo tres años estudiando español en el colegio. ¿Estudias inglés en el colegio?**
soy day **lon**-*dress,* **pe**-*ro a-o-ra* **bee**-*bo en* **gloss**-*ter. ess-***ta ther**-*ka day* **bree**-*stol.*
ye-*bo tress* **an**-*yoss ess-too-dee-***an**-*do ess-pan-***yol** *en el ko-***lekh**-*yo. ess-***too**-*dee-as*
*een-***gless** *en el ko-***lekh**-*yo?*
I'm from London, but now I live in Gloucester. It's near Bristol. I've spent three years studying Spanish at school. Do you study English at school?

Juanjo **Sí, y también francés. Lo estudio desde hace dos años, pero no lo hablo bien**
*see, ee tamb-***yen** *fran-***thess***. lo ess-***too**-*dee-o* **dess**-*day* **ath**-*ay dos* **an**-*yoss,* **pe**-*ro no lo* **ab**-*lo byen*
Yes, and French too. I've been studying it for two years, but I don't speak it well

Katy **Yo tampoco**
*yo tam-***po**-*ko*
Nor do I (me neither)

Two kinds of being

So far we've seen a lot of the word estar meaning 'to be'. But as you may know, one of the peculiarities of Spanish is that there are two different sorts of 'to be'. Here we have the other one, ser. This difference can be puzzling at first but after a while you'll start to recognise the principle behind it. Basically estar is for saying how or where something or someone is, while ser identifies it or describes its inherent nature. So you use ser for giving such things as your name (not age, for reasons explained below), nationality, profession and the place you come from. For giving the location of something it's estar, even if the thing is very permanently located there; so Gloucester está cerca de Bristol. Here's an example of the difference in action: es moreno means 'he's dark-skinned' but está moreno would be 'he's tanned'; eres guapa 'you're nice-looking' estás guapa 'you're looking nice'.

Age concerns

In Spanish age is expressed differently – instead of saying 'I am 13, you say the equivalent of 'I have 13 years'. So tengo trece años means 'I am thirteen'. If you were to translate literally, 'I'm 13' would be soy trece, but that's not what you say in Spanish. In English you 'are' a certain age, but in Spanish you have a certain number of years: tengo trece años 'I have thirteen years'. You can't drop the word for 'years' as you would in English. To ask someone their age, you say ¿cuántos años tienes?, literally 'how many years do you have?'

Naming names

There's a trick to giving your name, too. While it is possible to say mi nombre es … 'my name is', or just say 'I'm …' as Juanjo does (soy Juanjo), what people mostly say is me llamo …, literally 'I call myself …'. (If you know French, it's just like *je m'appelle*.) This is what's called a reflexive verb, meaning that the person or thing that does the action is also on the receiving end of it, they do it 'to themselves'. > Reflexive Verbs RefZone 33

> Reflexive Verbs RefZone 33

---

from the dialogue

¿cómo te llamas?
ko-mo tay ya-mass?
what's your name?

me llamo …
may ya-mo …
my name is …

tengo trece años
ten-go treth-ay an-yoss
I'm 13 years old

¿de dónde eres?
day don-day e-ress?
where are you from?

estoy de vacaciones
ess-toy day ba-kath-yon-ess
I'm on holiday

con
kon
with

mis padres
meess pa-dress
my parents

vivo en …
bee-bo en …
I live in …

desde hace …
dess-day ath-ay …
for …, since

yo tampoco
yo tam-po-ko
me neither

For and since

In English you can say 'I've been learning French for two years', or 'I started learning French two years ago'. The first describes how long an action has been going on; the second says when the action started. In Spanish the word desde 'from, since' is the key here, used with the present tense: estudio francés desde noviembre 'I've been learning French since November'; estudio francés desde hace dos años 'I've been learning French for two years'. The word hace is literally 'it makes'; turning it round you can say hace dos años que estudio francés, literally 'it makes two years that I've been studying French'. Another way of saying how long something has been happening is to use the verb llevar, which usually means to 'carry': llevo tres años estudiando español 'I've been learning Spanish for three years', llevo veinte minutos aquí 'I've been here for twenty minutes'.

Pet names

You may be wondering what sort of a name Juanjo is. In fact it's a sort of pet name, a contraction of Juan José. There are quite a few of these in Spanish: Chema for José María, Maite for María Teresa and so on. Straightforward shortenings include Tere for Teresa, Rafa for Rafael, while others are less easily guessable: Paco for Francisco, Pepe for José.

The -ing word

So what's this estudiando? That -ando is the Spanish equivalent of the English '-ing' ending. It's -iendo instead for -er and -ir verbs. Just as in English, you can combine it with the verb 'to be' (estar in this case) to give a present continuous tense: estudio – estoy estudiando 'I study – I am studying'. Easy!
> Verbs RefZone 19

Me too, me neither

You know that bien means 'well'. 'As well' translates almost literally into Spanish: tan 'as, so' + bien 'well' = también. The opposite, 'neither', is tampoco, literally 'as little'. So when Katy replies that her French isn't good either, she doesn't need to include the verb as we do in English ('nor do I, nor did she, nor will they', etc), she just puts the word yo 'me' with tampoco to make 'me neither'.

Mind your languages

There's a nice easy pattern here. Just as in English, the adjective associated with a given country is also the same as the name of the language. For example, inglés 'English', francés 'French', español 'Spanish', alemán 'German' and so on (languages are masculine). You can also use these nouns to mean a man from the country in question: un inglés 'an Englishman', un español 'a Spanish man', un alemán 'a German'. To refer to a woman from the particular country , change -és to -esa, -ol to -ola and -án to -ana. Thus una inglesa 'an Englishwoman', una española 'a Spanishwoman' and una alemana 'a German woman'.

My word!

Surprise, surprise, the word for 'my' varies according to who you're talking about. It's mi abuela 'my grandmother' but mis padres 'my parents'. But the good news is that for once there's no distinction between masculine and feminine, just mi for singular and mis for plural. For the equivalents for other people ('your', 'his/her' etc) > Possessives RefZone 12

Fatherland

Yes, it's 'men rule OK' again: your mum and dad collectively are your padres 'fathers', although of course it could mean 'fathers' as well. Likewise, tíos can mean 'uncles', 'aunt and uncle' or 'aunts and uncles'; hermanos can mean 'brothers', 'brother and sister' or 'brothers and sisters' and hijos can mean 'sons', 'son and daughter' or 'sons and daughters'. If someone refers to their children as mis hijos, it doesn't necessarily mean they only have sons.

The object of the exercise

Estudio francés. I'm studying French. Lo estudio desde hace dos años. I've been studying *it* for two years. So here 'it' is lo. It's what's known technically as a direct object pronoun, the word that replaces the name of the thing in the sentence that has something done to it. Of course, that's just the masculine singular one. Here are the others: la (feminine), los (masculine plural), las (feminine plural). > Pronouns RefZone 18

now practise

9

> **asking questions**

Asking the way

get to know ...

> directions
> imperatives
> numbers
> si/sí

Agustín **Oiga, por favor. ¿Por dónde se va a la Plaza Mayor? ¿Está muy lejos?**
oy-ga por fa-bor. por don-day say ba a la plath-a ma-yor? ess-ta mwee lay-khoss?
Excuse me please. How do you get to the Plaza Mayor (main square)? Is it very far?

Sergio **No. Está en el centro. Es fácil llegar, pero si quiere, puede coger un taxi**
no. ess-ta en el then-tro. ess fa-theel ye-gar, pe-ro see kyer-ay, pwed-ay ko-kher oon tak-see
No. It's in the town centre. It's easy to get there, but if you want you can take a taxi

Agustín **No importa, prefiero ir andando**
no eem-por-ta, pre-fyer-o eer an-dan-do
It doesn't matter, I prefer to walk (to go on foot)

Sergio **Pues siga todo recto por aquí. Luego coja la primera calle a la izquierda, y siga recto hasta el Ayuntamiento. Justo detrás está la Plaza Mayor**
pwess see-ga to-do rek-to por a-kee. lweg-o ko-kha la pree-may-ra ka-yay a la eeth-kyer-da, ee see-ga rek-to ass-ta el a-yoon-tam-yen-to. khoos-to de-trass ess-ta la plath-a ma-yor
Well, go straight on this way. Then take the first street on the left and then continue on as far as the Ayuntamiento (town hall). The Plaza Mayor is right behind

Agustín **Un momento, entonces sigo recto, luego a la izquierda y detrás del Ayuntamiento**
oon mo-men-to, en-tonth-ess see-go to-do rek-to, lweg-o a la eeth-kyer-da ee de-trass del a-yoon-tam-yen-to
Just a moment. So I go straight on, to the left and behind the Ayuntamiento

Sergio **Eso es**
ess-o ess
That's it

Agustín **Vale, muchas gracias. ¿Y el museo queda cerca de la plaza?**
ba-lay, moo-tchas grath-yass. ee el moo-say-o ke-da ther-ka de la plath-a?
OK, thanks very much. And is the museum near the square?

Sergio	**Sí, está a la derecha al lado de la iglesia** *see, ess-**ta** a la de-**re**-tcha al **la**-do day la ee-**gless**-ya* Yes, it's on the right, next to the church
Agustín	**Gracias** **grath**-yass Thanks
Sergio	**De nada. Adiós** *day **na**-da. ad-**yoss*** Not at all. Goodbye

from the dialogue

¿por dónde se va a ...?
*por **don**-day say ba a ...?*
how do you get to ...?

¿está lejos?
*es-**ta lay**-khos?*
is it far?

es facil
*ess **fa**-theel*
it's easy

no importa
*no eem-**por**-ta*
it doesn't matter

ir andando
*eer an-**dan**-do*
to walk/to go on foot

todo recto
***to**-do **rek**-to*
straight on

la primera calle
*la pree-**may**-ra **ka**-yay*
the first street

a la izquierda
*a la eeth-**kyer**-da*
on the left

detrás de ...
*de-**trass** de ...*
behind ...

¡eso es!
***ess**-o ess!*
that's it!

a la derecha
*a la de-**re**-tcha*
on the right

al lado de ...
*al **la**-do day ...*
beside/next to ...

Oy again

Remember that word oye 'listen!' we had earlier? This is just the usted form of it. It's a very common way of getting people's attention: ¡oiga! excuse me!

One to remember

'How do you get to ...?' we might ask in English, meaning how does a person get there, one, anyone – not specifically the person we're talking to. In Spanish you use – or 'one' uses – an 'impersonal' form, se. It takes the same verb endings as he, she or it. ¿Por dónde se va a la Plaza Mayor?

See?

It may seem like a nuisance to add accents to letters, but don't make the mistake of thinking they're optional or just decorative. Accents are used for two reasons in Spanish: most of the time to show where the stress falls in the pronunciation of a word, but sometimes to show the difference between two common words which would otherwise be indistinguishable in writing. That's why sí meaning 'yes', gets an accent, while si meaning 'if' is without. ¿Sabe usted si es éste el autobús que va al centro? – ¡sí!

-ing again

You'll see that -ando form again: prefiero ir andando 'I prefer to walk' – literally it's 'I prefer to go walking'. > Verbs RefZone 19

A command performance

¡Siga todo recto! ¡Coja la primera calle a la izquierda! We see lots of instructions given in this dialogue, using the formal usted endings rather than the familiar tú, since Augustín starts the conversation with that using oiga rather than oye. There are of course different command (imperative) endings for tu, usted, vosotros and ustedes. > Verbs RefZone 19

Got your number

There are two types of numbers, the ones you use to count with 'one, two, three', (known as cardinals) and the ones that tell you the order of things 'first, second, third' (known as ordinals), as in 'the first on the left' la primera calle a la izquierda. In Spanish they start off like this: uno–primer(o/a); dos–segundo(a); tres–tercer(o/a) – but you can get the whole story in the Reference Zone.

Location, location, location

We've seen that estar, rather than ser, is the verb to use when specifying the location of something. You can use the verb quedar in just the same way: el museo queda cerca de la plaza.

now practise

11

> **understanding directions**

At a café

12

> **get to know ...**
>
> > ustedes
> > emphatice pronouns
> > indirect object pronouns

Waiter **Hola, ¿qué van a tomar?**
*o-la, kay ban a to-**mar**?*
Hello, what are you going to have?

Valle **A mí me pone un café con leche, por favor. Tú ¿qué quieres, Lydia?**
*a mee may **po**-nay oon ka-**fay** kon **letch**-ay, por fa-**bor**. too kay **kyer**-ess, **leed**-ya?*
Bring *me* a white coffee (coffee with milk), please. What would *you* like, Lydia?

Lydia **Yo quiero agua mineral**
*yo **kyer**-o **ag**-wa mee-nay-**ral***
I want mineral water

Waiter **¿Con o sin gas?**
kon o seen gas?
Sparkling or still?

Lydia **Sin gas. Me trae el vaso sin hielo, por favor**
*seen gas. may **tra**-ay el **ba**-so seen **yay**-lo, por fa-**bor***
Still. Please bring me the glass without ice

Waiter **Claro**
***kla**-ro*
Of course

Valle **¿Me puede traer sacarina, por favor?**
*may **pwed**-ay tra-**er** sa-ka-**ree**-na, por fa-**bor**?*
Can you bring me some sweetener, please?

Waiter **No hay problema, enseguida les traigo todo**
*no aee prob-**lem**-a, en-se-**gee**-da layss **traee**-go **tod**-o*
No problem, I'll bring it all right away

(later)

Waiter **Aquí tienen**
*a-**kee tyen**-en*
Here you are

Lydia	**Gracias. ¿Cuánto es todo?**
	grath-yass. kwan-to ess tod-o?
	Thanks. How much is it altogether?
Waiter	**Son cinco ochenta**
	son theen-ko otch-en-ta
	It's 5 euros 80
Lydia	**Aquí tiene**
	a-kee tyen-ay
	Here you are

Put it there

That word poner is a very useful verb when asking to be given or brought things. It basically means 'to put', but here we'd have to translate it as 'get me' or 'bring me' a coffee.

The return of the pronouns!

We stated early on that Spanish tends to drop the pronoun in sentences where it's not really required, because (unlike in English) it's easy to tell who is doing what from the verb ending. ¿Qué quieres? just means 'what do you want?' So if we add in that neglected pronoun tú, the effect is much the same as if we'd emphasised the 'you' in English using a different tone of voice: tú ¿qué quieres? 'what do *you* want?' And the same thing happens in the reply: Yo quiero agua mineral '*I'd* like a mineral water' (whereas *you're* having coffee). It's the same yo that we saw earlier in the phrase yo tampoco 'me neither, nor do I'. Obviously where there's no verb present, you can't just go by the verb ending!

from the dialogue

me pone ...
may po-nay ...
can I have ...? /bring me ...

un café con leche
oon ka-fay kon letch-ay
a white coffee

un agua mineral
oon ag-wa mee-nay-ral
a mineral water

con gas
kon gass
sparkling

sin gas
seen gass
still

me trae ...
may tra-ay ...
please bring me ...

el vaso
el ba-so
the glass

no hay problema
no aee prob lem a
no problem

enseguida
en-se-gee-da
straight away

¿cuánto es?
kwan-to ess?
how much is it?

todo
tod-o
all

Me me me!

Just as you can say Yo quiero to be more explicit than just quiero, you can use an emphatic pronoun with actions that happen *to* you: a mí me pone un café '*I'll* have a coffee' – with the implication 'but what about *you*, Lydia?' There are different pronouns for this. > Pronouns RefZone 18

Gimme gimme gimme

Yo quiero agua mineral, says Lydia. This would sound pretty demanding in English if translated literally: 'I want a mineral water!' Same with the blunt-seeming statement me pone un agua mineral 'you (will) get me a mineral water'. It sounds OK in Spanish!

Two types of object

We've seen how to translate 'it' when it's the 'direct' object of the action of a sentence, eg 'I've been studying it' (studying French, that is). But a sentence can have two objects. If you say me trae el vaso 'bring me the glass', both you and the glass are objects of the action in different ways, the glass being the 'direct' one, the one that's most fundamental to the meaning of the sentence. After all you could say 'bring the glass' and the meaning would still be the same, but 'bring me' would change things totally. > Pronouns RefZone 18

Youse guys

¿Qué van a tomar? asks the waiter, and enseguida les traigo todo. It might look as if he's saying 'What are *they* going to have?' and 'I'll bring it to *them*' instead of 'you'. That's because he's addressing the customers as ustedes, the plural of usted, the polite or formal word for 'you'. Just as usted takes the endings associated with 'he, she, it', so logically enough the plural form ustedes has the same endings as 'they'. > Verbs RefZone 19

See you later, peseta!

In Britain and America prices are expressed in two units of currency: pounds and pence, and dollars and cents. Notice that the verb ser 'to be' agrees with the amount expressed; whereas in English we'd say 'it *is* 5 euros', in Spanish they *are* 5 euros: son 5 euros. In the days of pesetas, there was only one unit, since the peseta was so small, but now the euro is here, so you give the euros followed by the number of cents: son cinco ochenta 'it's five euros eighty'. Sometimes people use the word con 'with': son cinco con ochenta. In English the word 'cent' covers both euros and dollars, but in Spanish there are different words: 100 céntimos in a euro, but 100 centavos in a dollar.

Here you have it

The verb tener is often used when handing things over to people. Phrases like aquí tiene and ahí tiene are equivalent to 'here/there you are' or 'go, and you can use them with the name of the thing you're handing over too: aquí tiene el café 'here's your coffee'. > Tener RefZone 26

Meeting family

get to know ...
> vosotros
> preterite and perfect
> deminutives
> subjunctive

Esther **Tony, te presento a mi abuela, Marisa. Vive en Zaragoza pero ha venido a pasar unos días con nosotros**
to-nee, tay pre-**sen**-to a mee ab-**wel**-a, ma-**ree**-sa. **bee**-bay en tha-ra-**go**-tha **pe**-ro a ben-**ee**-do a pa-**sar** oo-noss **dee**-ass kon no-**so**-tross
Tony, meet my grandmother, Marisa. She lives in Zaragoza but she's come to spend a few days with us

Tony **Hola, encantado. ¿Cómo está usted?**
o-la, en-kan-**ta**-do. **ko**-mo ess-**ta** oo-**sted**?
Hello, nice to meet you, how are you?

Marisa **Bien, gracias. ¿Estás de vacaciones?**
byen, **grath**-yass. ess-**tas** day ba-kath-**yon**-ess?
Fine, thanks. Are you on holiday?

Tony **Sí, soy inglés y he venido a pasar un mes en España**
see, soy een-**gless** ee ay be-**nee**-do a pa-**sar** oon mess en ess-**pan**-ya
Yes, I'm English and I've come to spend a month in Spain

Marisa **Hablas muy bien el español. ¿Dónde lo has aprendido?**
ab-lass mwee buen el ess-pan-**yol**. **don**-day lo ass a-pren-**dee**-do?
You speak very good Spanish. Where did you learn it?

Tony **Gracias. Estudié español dos años en la universidad**
grath-yass. ess-**tood**-yay ess-pan-**yol** doss **an**-yoss en la oo-nee-ber-see-**dad**
Thanks. I studied Spanish for two years at university

Marisa **¿Te gusta España?**
tay **goo**-sta ess-**pan**-ya?
Do you like Spain?

Tony **Sí, mucho. En Inglaterra hace mucho frío, y como me encanta el sol ...**
see, **moo**-tcho. en eeng-la-**ter**-ra **ath**-ay **moo**-tcho **free**-o, ee **ko**-mo may en-**kan**-ta el sol ...
Yes, I like it a lot. In England it's very cold, and as I love the sun ...

Marisa **Es verdad, aquí hace más calor, pero hay que tener cuidado con el sol, sobre todo en la playa**
*ess ber-**dad**, a-**kee ath**-ay mass ka-**lor**, **pe**-ro aee kay ten-**er** kwee-**da**-do kon el sol, **so**-bray **tod**-o en la **pla**-ya*
That's true, it's hotter here, but you have to be careful with the sun, especially on the beach

Esther **Abuela, que ya no somos niños**
*a-**bwe**-la, kay ya no **so**-moss **neen**-yoss*
Granny, we're not kids any mor

Tony **Es verdad, hay que tener cuidado. El año pasado mi hermano cogió una insolación y estuvo muy malo**
*ess ber-**dad**, aee kay ten-**er** kwee-**da**-do. el **an**-yo pa-**sa**-do mee er-**ma**-no kokh-**yo oo**-na een-so-lath-**yon** ee ess-**too**-bo mwee **mal**-o*
It's true, you have to be careful. Last year my brother got sunstroke and was very ill

Marisa **Además, los ingleses tenéis la piel muy clara y os quemáis enseguida. Es más peligroso para vosotros**
*a-day-**mass**, loss een-**gless**-ess ten-**ay**-eess la pyel mwee **kla**-ra ee oss ke-**ma**-yeess en-seg-**ee**-da. es mass pe-lee-**gro**-so **pa**-ra bos-**o**-tross*
Also, you English have very pale skin and you burn straight away. It's more dangerous for you

Esther **Bueno, abuelita, nos vamos a la playa. Hasta luego**
***bwen** o, ab-wel-**ee**-ta, noss **ba**-moss a la **pla**-ya. **ass**-ta **lweg**-o*
OK, Granny, we're off to the beach. Bye!

Tony **Adiós, señora. Encantado**
*ad-**yoss**, sen-**yo**-ra. en-kan-**ta**-do*
Goodbye. Nice to meet you

Marisa **Hasta luego, que lo paséis bien**
***ass**-ta **lweg**-o, ke lo pa-**sayss** byen*
See you, have a nice time

Charmed I'm sure

¿Te gusta España? means 'do you like Spain?' But notice that the the expression is the other way round to English: you don't 'like' a thing, it 'pleases' you, with the pleasing thing as the subject of the verb rather than the person it pleases. A stronger version of this is encantar(a), literally 'to enchant': me encanta el sol 'I love the sun'. It's the same verb we see in the expression you use when you meet someone: encantado, short for encantado de conocerle, 'delighted to meet you'.

A perfect past

In English we have two ways of putting a sentence into the past, by changing the verb itself 'I did it' or using the verb 'to have', as in 'I have done it'. The same is true in Spanish: just take the relevant part of the verb haber, and add the main verb (in a form known as the past participle) and you get he venido. That -ido ending (-ado for -ar verbs) stays the same whoever is involved, just as in English 'come' is the same whether it's 'I have come' or 'he has come'. This tense is called the perfect. The other past tense, the one that reminds you of 'I did it', is called the preterite. Compare dónde lo has aprendido (perfect) with estudié español (preterite). If it had been the other way round we'd have had dónde lo aprendiste (preterite) and he estudiado español (perfect). The meaning is more or less the same, but the form is different. You might find one easier to use than the other. In the Reference Zone we show you how to form these tenses with various different verbs. > Verbs RefZone 19

Making heavy weather of it

In English it 'is' hot or cold. In Spanish the word hace is used, literally it 'makes' or 'does', with a noun instead of an adjective: ¡hace calor/frío! 'it's hot/cold!' Because it's a noun not an adjective in Spanish 'heat', not 'hot', you intensify it with mucho and not with muy, so 'it's very cold' is hace mucho frío. Again, you use the noun rather than the adjective to say you're feeling hot or cold: tengo calor/frio 'I'm hot/cold', literally 'I have heat/cold'. The same applies to other feelings: tengo hambre/sed 'I'm hungry/thirsty'.

Hot and hotter

To say that something is bigger, *more* interesting, or whatever, couldn't be much easier. You just use the word más 'more', as in más peligroso 'more dangerous'. The opposite, '*less* dangerous', is menos. Just as in English, there are exceptions, like bueno–mejor (good–better rather than 'gooder'). The good news is you don't have to worry why it's 'more interesting' not 'interestinger' or why 'bigger' sounds better than 'more big'. For superlatives 'biggest', 'most interesting' it's the same word más, with the article el or la before it: el más grande 'the biggest' (masculine), la más interesante 'the most interesting' (feminine).

Gotta be done

We've seen the word hay meaning 'there is...' or 'there are...': ¿hay un hotel por aquí cerca? no hay problema. If you follow it with que you get a very useful construction meaning 'it is necessary to', 'you have to': hay que tener cuidado 'you have to be careful'.

You, ya, yous, y'all, you guys...

So just how many words are there in Spanish for 'you'? We've seen usted, the formal singular, and its plural ustedes, and we've seen the informal word tú; now here is its plural, vosotros. What's interesting here is that while Marisa calls her granddaughter's friend Tony tú, as we'd expect, she also uses the vosotros form at one point: los ingleses tenéis la piel muy clara y os quemáis enseguida. This is because in referring to the English generally ('all you English people' not just 'you, Tony') she has to use the plural of tú rather than usted, even though she's including people she wouldn't actually address as tú if she met them!

Little old ladies

What's this word abuelita? It's just abuela 'grandmother' with an ending called the diminutive, which changes the feel of the word slightly. Sometimes it means that the thing is physically smaller, often it just makes the word more affectionate or polite – un poquito 'a little bit', un momentito 'a wee moment'. However, many diminutives have become set expressions with specific meanings. For example a carrito is not just a small carro 'cart', but a shopping trolley. It's a bit like the English word 'cigarette', which is not just a smaller version of a cigar. The most common diminutive ending is -ito (-ita for the feminine) but there are various others as well, such as -illo, -ino and -ico.

Sub what?

In the phrase que lo paséis bien we see a form of the verb we haven't mentioned before, called the subjunctive. The term may sound obscure and technical but it is very much part of everyday Spanish. It's typically used in hypothetical or potential situations, such as desires and wishes. It's often found following the word que 'that', where the sense is often captured by the English word 'should', 'may' or 'let': ' It can also be used to translate 'let's': ¡bailemos! 'let's dance!'; ¡comamos! let's eat! > VERBS REFZONE 19

now practise
> using ser and estar

At a restaurant

> **future tense**
> **por and para**

Cristina **Hola, una mesa para dos, por favor**
o-la, *oo*-na **mess**-a **pa**-ra doss por fa-**bor**
Hello, a table for two please

Waiter **Hola, pasen por aquí, por favor. Aquí tienen la carta**
o-la, **pa**-sen por a-**kee**, por fa-**bor**. a-**kee tyen**-en la **kar**-ta
Hello, come this way please. Here's the menu

(later)

Waiter **¿Saben ya qué van a tomar?**
sa-ben ya kay ban a **tom**-ar?
Are you ready to order? (Do you know yet what you are going to have?)

Leandro **Sí, yo tomaré de primero una sopa de verduras, y de segundo me gustaría un filete a la pimienta, por favor**
see, yo to-ma-**ray** day pree-**may**-ro **oo**-na **so**-pa day ber-**doo**-rass, ee day se-**goon**-do may goo-sta-**ree**-a oon fee-**let**-ay a la peem-**yen**-ta, por fa-**bor**
Yes, I'll have vegetable soup for my first course, and for the second (main) course I'd like a pepper steak, please

Waiter **¿Y usted que va a tomar?**
ee oo-**sted** kay ba a **tom**-ar?
And what will *you* have?

Cristina **Yo tomaré de primero una ensalada, y de segundo me apetece una chuleta**
yo tom-a-**ray** day pree-**may**-ro **oo**-na en-sa-**la**-da, ee day se-**goon**-do may a-pet-**eth**-ay **oo**-na tchoo-**let**-a
I'll have for my first course a salad, and for my second course I fancy a chop

Waiter **¿Qué van a tomar de beber?**
kay ban a **tom**-ar day beb-**er**?
What will you have to drink?

Leandro **Tráiganos una botella de vino tinto de la casa**
traee-ga-noss **oo**-na bo-**te**-ya day **bee**-no **teen**-to day la **ka**-sa
Bring us a bottle of red house wine

Waiter	**Muy bien**	
	mwee byen	
	Very well	

(later)

Waiter	**¿Quieren tomar algún postre?**
	kyer-en tom-ar al-goon post-ray?
	Do you want a dessert?

Cristina	**No, gracias. ¿Nos trae la cuenta, por favor?**
	no, grath-yass. nos tra-ay la kwen-ta, por fa-bor?
	No thanks. Will you bring us the bill, please?

Waiter	**Aquí tienen**
	a-kee tyen-en
	Here you are

did you know ...?

Mealtimes are different in Spain to what we're used to. The midday meal is often well into the afternoon, any time from 1pm to about 3pm. As for the evening meal, it's more a night-time affair, perhaps three hours later than a British family might be tucking in. 8pm is normal, 10 or 11 nothing unusual, especially in Madrid. The 'madrileños' are famous for being night-birds and wouldn't think of setting out for a night on the town before 10 o'clock!

In no particular order

You may be fed up with the fact that there are so many endings in Spanish, and the way everything seems to have to 'agree' with something. To put it informally, Spanish has 'a lot of grammar' compared to English. But once you have learned the endings they are generally very logical and predictable. Another result of all this 'grammar' is that the word order can often be very free: ¿usted qué va a tomar? is much the same as ¿qué va a tomar usted? or ¿qué va usted a tomar?

Going into the future

We've seen that there is more than one way of forming a past tense, one of them involving using the verb haber rather like the way the verb 'to have' can be used in English. The same applies to the future. As well as the standard future tense endings, you can also express future ideas using ir 'to go', just as we do in English, and the two can appear side by side: ¿qué van a tomar? – tomaré una ensalada 'what are you going to have? – I'll have a salad'.
> Ir RefZone 28

Tickling your fancy

Here's another construction, like gustar and encantar, that works the other way to English. Me apetece un café means 'I fancy a coffee', literally 'a coffee tempts (or entices) me'.

Horses for courses

Notice the use of the word de for different parts of the meal. You could order by just naming the things you want: de primero such and such, de segundo something else and de beber to specify a drink. The standard pattern in Spain is the primer plato 'first dish', usually something light such as a soup, followed by the segundo plato 'second dish', typically meat or fish. These two are the basis of the meal; a dessert (postre) may follow, and it's this rather than the starter which is seen as an optional extra. A basket of bread is provided as a matter of course. Vegetables are considered separately, so each course may consist of just one item, such as a piece of meat, rather than a selection of things as in Britain, although the plato combinado meat or fish with rice, potatoes or chips and vegetables is widely available particularly in tourist areas.

Por and para

It's easy to get confused between por and para. Though por sounds more like English *for* and French *pour* than para does, it's actually para that's closer to the meaning of 'for', as well as 'to' or 'in order to': una mesa para dos 'a table for two', un billete para Madrid 'a ticket for Madrid', te llamo mañana para ver como estás 'I'll call you tomorrow to see how you are'. As for por, it has various meanings, covering such things as 'through', 'by way of' and 'because of': gracias por ... 'thanks for ...', ¿por dónde se va a ...? 'how do you get to ...?', por aquí 'this way', por el parque 'through the park', el precio por noche 'the price per night'. There are lots of set expressions too: por favor 'please', por cierto 'by the way', por supuesto 'of course' and so on.

> PREPOSITIONS REFZONE 14

You do this, please

We see plenty of command (imperative) forms in this section, with customers and waiter giving each other instructions: pasen por aquí 'come this way', tráiganos una botella 'bring us a bottle' – but notice that where the context is clear you can also give instructions using the good old present tense: ¿Nos trae la cuenta, por favor? A handy 'cheat'!

breakfast
el desayuno
*el dess-a-**yoo**-no*

lunch
el almuerzo
*el alm-**werth**-o*

dinner (evening)
la cena
*la **then**-a*

to have breakfast
desayunar
*dess-a-yoo-**nar***

to have lunch
comer
*ko-**mer***

to have dinner
cenar
*then-**ar***

the menu
la carta
*la **kar**-ta*

the set menu
el menú
*el men-**oo***

the dish of the day
el plato del día
*el **plu**-to del **dee**-a*

fried
frito(a)
***freet**-o(a)*

roasted
asado(a)
*ass-**a**-do(a)*

grilled
a la parrilla
*a la pa-**ree**-a*

baked
al horno
*al **or**-no*

Shopping

get to know ...

> accented letters
> quantities

Shopkeeper **Buenas tardes, ¿qué desea?**
*bwen-ass **tar**-dess, kay de-**say**-a?*
Good afternoon, what would you like?

Belén **Quería doscientos gramos de jamón serrano**
*ke-**ree**-a doss **thyen**-toss **gra**-moss day kha-**mon** ser-**ra**-no*
I'd like 200 grammes of cured ham

Shopkeeper **¿Le pongo algo más?**
*lay **pon**-go **al**-go mass?*
Anything else? (Shall I get you anything more?)

Belén **Sí, un cuarto de jamón de York, por favor**
*see, oon **kwar**-to day kha-**mon** day york, por fa-**bor***
Yes, a quarter of cooked ham, please

Shopkeeper **Aquí tiene**
*a-**kee tyen**-ay*
Here you are

Belén **Póngame también un cuarto de aceitunas y un trozo de queso Manchego**
*pon-ga-me tamb-**yen** oon **kwar**-to day a-thay-**too**-nass ee oon **tro**-tho day **kay**-so man-**tcheg**-o*
And give me also a quarter-kilo of olives and a piece of Manchego cheese

Shopkeeper **Muy bien. ¿Qué más le pongo? Tengo melocotones, naranjas, peras, manzanas ...**
*mwee byen. kay mass lay **pon**-go? **ten**-go mel-o-ko-**to**-ness, na-**ran**-khass, **pe**-rass, man-**tha**-nass ...*
Very good. What else shall I get you? I've got peaches, oranges, pears, apples ...

Belén **Póngame un kilo de naranjas y medio de melocotones**
*pon-ga-may oon **kee**-lo day na-**ran**-khass ee **med**-yo day mel-o-ko-**to**-ness*
(Get me) a kilo of oranges and a half-kilo of peaches

Shopkeeper **¿Algo más?**
***al**-go mass?*
Anything else?

Belén	**No, eso es todo, gracias. ¿Cuánto es?**
	*no, **es**-o es **to**-do, **grath**-yass. **kwan**-to ess?*
	No, that's all thanks. How much is it?
Shopkeeper	**Son doce euros**
	*Son **doth**-ay **eoo**-ros*
	It's 12 euros
Belén	**Aquí tiene. Adiós**
	*a-**kee tyen**-ay. ad-**yoss***
	Here you are. Goodbye
Shopkeeper	**Gracias, adiós**
	grath**-yass, ad-**yoss
	Thanks, goodbye

from the dialogue

¿qué desea?
*kay de-**say**-a?*
what would you like?

quería ...
*ke-**ree**-a ...*
I'd like ...

jamón Serrano
*kha-**mon** ser-**ra**-no*
cured ham

¿algo más?
***al**-go mass?*
anything else?

jamón de York
*kha-**mon** day york*
cooked ham

póngame ...
***pon**-ga-me ...*
give me ...

un cuarto de ...
*oon **kwar**-to day ...*
a quarter-kilo of ...

un trozo de ...
*oon **troth**-o day ...*
a piece of ...

medio de ...
***med**-yo day ...*
a half-kilo of ...

eso es todo
*ess-o ess **tod**-o*
that's all

Open all hours?

¡Buenas tardes! says the shopkeeper. We often translate this as 'good afternoon', but it doesn't correspond exactly. It often translates as evening. You need to bear in mind that for cultural (and climatic reasons) the concept of the afternoon is different in Spain. In Spain the working day is traditionally divided into two by a long lunch-hour, and, in hotter parts of the country, a siesta, although the jornada continua or intensiva (no lunchbreak) is becoming more common. Smaller shops and offices usually close for lunch at about 1.30 or 2pm and reopen at 4 or even later. The tarde starts at lunchtime, whenever that's taken, and carries on till the end of the day, say 8pm or so. After that it's buenas noches, for greeting as well as saying goodbye, So don't be surprised to be wished what seeems like 'good morning' at 1pm, or 'good afternoon' at 7.30pm, or greeted with 'goodnight'!

What shall I put you?

There are lots of ways of asking for something in shops, restaurants and so on. A simple quiero 'I want' is one; it doesn't sound rude in Spanish, but if you want a less direct way of putting it there's also quería or quisiera 'I would like'. Or you can use the verb poner, as we saw in the café dialogue. Qué le pongo? the customer is asked, 'what shall I 'put' you?' The imperative (command form) is ponga when you're talking to someone as usted (or pon in the informal tú form), and you'll notice that the part corresponding to 'me' or 'us' or whatever 'put *me* some...' gets welded onto the end of the verb: póngame un kilo de naranjas.

Accentuate the difference

This tacking on of extra words in the command form (ponga + me = póngame) has an effect on the spelling too. The general rule about accents showing how to stress a word is that if the stress comes on the last syllable, or the next-to-last in cases where the word ends in a vowel or n or s, there's no need to mark it. That's fine for ponga. But when you add an extra syllable (-me), the stress stays on the pon part, which means the word no longer obeys the general rules about stress, and does need an accent. In fact it could even get another syllable again if we added something to mean 'it': póngamelo 'put me it'. If the stress of a word falls on the third from last (antepenultimate) syllable it will *always* need an accent.

¿Qué?

Another quick point about accents. When a word like que, quien, como, cuanto or donde asks a question, as opposed to just linking two ideas (hay que tener cuidado), it needs an accent: ¿qué?, ¿quién?, ¿cómo?, cuánto or ¿dónde? So, ¿Saben ya qué van a tomar? is 'do you know yet *what* you want to have?' but if you write the question without the accent it would, theoretically, mean 'do you know yet *that* you want to have something?' ¿Qué más? ¡Nada más!

Types of ham

In Spain ham is often cured ham, seasoned and air-dried before being served in very thin slices as a luxurious appetiser or garnish – similar to what we know in Britain as Parma ham. In Spanish it's called jamón serrano, 'mountain ham', because the best ham comes from high mountain areas where the air is cold and dry. The Spanish term for cooked ham of the sort that's usual in Britain is jamón de York 'York ham'.

a shop
una tienda
*oo-na **tyen**-da*

the butcher's
la carnicería
*la kar-neeth-er-**ee**-a*

the bakery
la panadería
*la pa-na-der-**ee**-a*

the fishmonger's
el carnicería
*la kar-neeth-e-**ree**-a*

a supermarket
un supermercado
*oon soo-per-mer-**ka**-do*

the grocer's
la tienda de ultramarinos
*la **tyen**-da day ool-tra-ma-**ree**-noss*

the tobacconist's
el estanco
*el ess-**tan**-ko*

the cake-shop
la pastelería
*la pass-tel-er-**ee**-a*

a bank
un banco
*oon **ban**-ko*

a cash dispenser
un cajero automático
*oon ka-**kher**-o aoo-tom-**a**-tee-ko*

Weighty matters

Quantities such as 'a kilo of' un kilo de, 'a litre of' un litro de, are always followed by de, never del, de las, de los, etc.
Its interesting to see that there are no apostrophes used within Spanish words (unlike in French, eg d'eau and Italian, eg d'arte) to indicate vanishing vowels. So it's something less to worry about!

Reporting a theft

Caroline **Quería denunciar un robo**
ke-**ree**-ya den-oonth-**yar** oon **rob**-o
I'd like to report a theft

Policeman **Dígame**
dee-ga-may
Tell me about it

Caroline **Me han robado el bolso**
may an rob-**a**-do el **bol**-so
My bag has been stolen

Policeman **¿Cómo ocurrió?**
ko-mo o-koor-**yo?**
How did it happen?

Caroline **Iba por el parque. Un hombre me pidió la hora, y de pronto, me quitó el bolso y salió corriendo**
ee-ba por el **par**-kay. oon **om**-bray may peed-**yo** la **o**-ra, ee day **pron**-to, may kee-**to** el **bol**-so ee sal-**yo** korr-**yen**-do
I was going through the park. A man asked me the time, and suddenly, he took my bag from me and ran off

Policeman **¿Cómo era el hombre? ¿Por dónde huyó?**
ko-mo **er**-a el **om**-bray? por **don**-day oo-**yo?**
What was the man like? Which way did he run off?

Caroline **Era bastante joven, alto, tenía el pelo negro y llevaba una camisa verde. Vi que se metió en la boca del metro**
e-ra bas-**tan**-tay kho-ben, **al**-to, te-**nee**-a el **pel**-o **neg**-ro ee ye-**ba**-ba **oo**-na ka-**mee**-sa **ber**-day. bee kay say met-**yo** en la la **bok**-a del **met**-ro
He was fairly young, tall, he had black hair and was wearing a green shirt. I saw him go into the entrance to the Underground

Policeman **¿Cómo es el bolso?**
ko-mo ess el **bol**-so?
What's the bag like?

Caroline **Marrón, de piel y con las iniciales CMS**
*mar-**ron**, day pyel ee kon lass ee-neeth-**ya**-less thay
ay-may **ess**-ay*
Brown, made of leather and with the initials CMS

Policeman **¿Qué llevaba dentro?**
*kay yay-**ba**-ba **dent**-ro?*
What were you carrying in it?

Caroline **¡Todo! La cartera, un billete de avión, mi móvil, una cámara digital y unos sesenta euros**
*tod-o! la kar-**tay**-ra, oon bee-**yet**-ay day ab-**yon**, mee **mo**-beel, **oo**-na ka-ma-ra dee-khee-**tal** ee **oo**-noss se-**sen**-ta **eoo**-ross*
Everything! My wallet, an airline ticket, my mobile phone, a digital camera and about 60 euros

Policeman **¿Me puede dar sus datos personales para rellenar el formulario?**
*me **pwed**-ay dar sooss **da**-toss per-so-**na**-less **pa**-ra re-yen-**ar** el for-moo-**lar**-yo?*
Can you give me your personal details in order to fill in this form?

Caroline **Sí, me llamo Caroline Smith. Soy británica, de Manchester**
*see, may **ya**-mo ka-ro-**laeen** es-**meeth**, soy bree-**ta**-nee-ka, day **mantch**-es-ter*
Yes, my name is Caroline Smith. I'm British, from Manchester

Policeman **¿Me enseña su carné de identidad o pasaporte?**
*may en-**sen**-ya soo kar-**nay** day ee-den-tee-**dad** o pa-sa-**por**-tay?*
Will you show me your identity card or passport?

Caroline **Lo siento, ¡no puedo! Es que también me lo han robado, lo llevaba en el bolso ...**
*lo **syen**-to, no **pwed**-o! ess kay tamb-**yen** may lo an ro-**ba**-do, lo ye-**ba**-ba en el **bol**-so ...*
I'm sorry, I can't! The thing is, that was stolen too, I was carrying it in the bag ...

from the dialogue

denunciar un robo
*den-oonth-**yar** oon **rob**-o*
to report a theft

idígame!
dee-ga-may!
yes?/tell me about it

me han robado el ...
*may an ro-**bad**-o el ...*
my ... has been stolen

¿cómo era?
*ko-mo **er**-a?*
what was he like?

¿por dónde?
*por **don**-day?*
which way?

tener el pelo negro
*ten-**er** el **pel**-o **neg**-ro*
to have black hair

¿cómo es ...?
ko-mo ess ...?
what is ... like?

sus datos personales
*soos **da**-tos per-so-**na**-less*
your personal details

¿me enseña ...?
*may en-**sen**-ya ...?*
will you show me ...?

lo siento
*lo **syen**-to*
I'm sorry

'Ello 'ello 'ello?

That word dígame comes from decir, to say or tell, plus the object pronoun me: 'tell me!' It's a very common way of telling someone to go ahead, you're listening. It's what people say when they pick up the phone, but you can use it in person too. Sometimes it's abbreviated to diga 'speak!' and if you were talking to someone you would address as tú, it would be di or dime.

'They' did it!

You may be puzzled to see that the victim of the robbery uses the plural – me han robado el bolso – even though the attacker was acting alone. This is because it doesn't really mean 'they stole my bag', more 'my bag was stolen' or 'someone stole my bag'.

Two types of past

There are different ways of talking about things that happened in the past. An action can be seen as, for example, a gradually ongoing thing, or a finished event that's over and done with. In English we can say either 'I was going' or 'I went': the action may be the same but you can view it differently. Here we have someone setting the scene ('I was going through the park') and then describing events ('a man asked me the time'). There is description ('he was wearing …') and action ('he took my bag'). We've seen the preterite and perfect tenses already; this new 'was doing' tense is known as the imperfect. You can find out about how to form it in the Reference Zone.

Cops and robbers

That verb robar might seem straightforward but it can be confusing. It doesn't always mean 'to rob' but also 'to steal' – in other words can refer to the thing stolen, as well as the person or place it was taken from.

Doing a runner

Do you remember prefiero ir andando in the dialogue about asking the way? The verb andar gives us andando 'walking', and here we have the same thing with correr 'to run, or hurry'. You take a verb such as 'go', 'leave', etc, and combine it with one that tells you how the motion was done (at a run, on foot, etc) with one of those -ando/-endo endings (gerund or 'present participle'). So salir corriendo is to 'run off' or 'rush away'; llegar andando would be 'to arrive on foot', and so on.

Ask away

Very often we find that one language has two words for the same thing, in other words there is a difference of meaning that doesn't exist in our own language. For example, the words preguntar and pedir both mean 'to ask', but it depends what you mean. You can ask a question (preguntar), or ask for a thing (pedir), which also works as the translation of 'to order' in shops and restaurants.

I feel for you

The usual Spanish phrase for 'I'm sorry' is lo siento, which literally means 'I feel it'. You can also say perdone (for usted) or perdona (for tú) from the verb perdonar 'to forgive', or get round the problem of which pronoun to choose by using the noun instead: perdón 'pardon'.

Choosing a colour

Colours used as adjectives must agree with the noun they are describing: el pelo negro 'black hair', una camisa verde 'a green shirt', el bolso marrón 'the brown handbag'. However, some colours are 'invariable' and never change, such as naranja 'orange' and rosa 'pink'. Note that the colour follows the noun rather than going in front of it as in English. > COLOURS REFZONE 8

extra vocabulary

a blue skirt
una falda azul
oo-na fal-da a-thool

a pink t-shirt
una camiseta rosa
oo-na ka-mee-set-a ross-a

a red blouse
una blusa roja
oo-na bloo-sa ro-kha

striped trousers
pantalones de rayas
pan-ta-lo-ness day ra-yass

black gloves
guantes negros
gwan-tess neg-ross

a white shirt
una camisa blanca
oo-na ka-mee-sa blan-ka

a brown jacket
una chaqueta marrón
oo-na tcha-ket-a mar-ron

some grey socks
unos calcetines grises
oo-noss kal-thet-ee-ness gree-sess

black knickers
bragas negras
bra-gass neg-rass

a red bra
un sujetador rojo
oon soo-khet-a-dor ro-kho

a pair of sandals
unas sandalias
oo-nass san-dal-yass

 now practise

> colours

At the station

get to know ...

> times
> comparatives
> adjectives before nouns
> cuál, este, ese, éste, ése

Marisa **Buenos días. Quería un billete para Madrid en el próximo tren, por favor**
*bwen-oss **dee**-ass. ke-**ree**-a oon bee-**yet**-ay **pa**-ra mad-**reed** en el **prok**-see-mo tren,
por fa-**bor***
Good morning. I'd like a ticket to Madrid on the next train, please

Assistant **¿De ida y vuelta?**
*day **ee**-da ee **bwel**-ta?*
Return?

Marisa **No, de ida. ¿A qué hora llega a Madrid?**
*no, day **ee**-da. a kay **o**-ra **ye**-ga a mad-**reed**?*
No, single. What time does it get to Madrid?

Assistant **Hay dos trenes: el primero es un AVE directo que sale a la una y llega
a Madrid a las dos cuarenta y cinco. El segundo es un TALGO que sale
a la una y cuarto y llega a las tres y veinte minutos. ¿Cuál quiere?**
*aee doss **tre**-ness: el pree-**may**-ro ess oon **a**-bay dee-**rek**-to ke **sa**-lay a la **oo**-na ee
ye-ga a mad-**reed** a lass doss kwa-**ren**-ta ee **theen**-ko. el se-**goon**-do ess oon **tal**-go
ke **sa**-lay a la **oo**-na ee **kwar**-to ee **ye**-ga a lass tress ee **bayn**-tay mee-**noo**-toss.
kwal **kyer**-ay?*
There are two trains: the first is a direct AVE which leaves at one and arrives in
Madrid at 2.45. The second is a TALGO which leaves at a quarter past one and
arrives at twenty past three. Which one do you want?

Marisa **Vamos a ver. El AVE es más rápido, ¿no? Deme un billete para el AVE de la una**
***ba**-moss a ber.el a-bay ess ma **ra**-pee-do, no? **dem**-ay oon bee-**yay**-tay **pa**-ra el **a**-bay
day la **oo**-na*
Let's see. The AVE is faster, isn't it? Give me a ticket for the one-o'clock AVE

Assistant **Sí, el AVE es el más rapido que tenemos. El billete de clase turista vale
cuarenta y cuatro euros, y el de preferente sesenta y cinco**
*see, el **a**-bay ess el ma **ra**-pee-do kay te-**ne**-moss. el bee-**yet**-ay day **kla**-say too-**ree**-sta
ba-lay kwa-**ren**-ta ee **kwa**-tro **eoo**-ross, ee el del pre-fe-**ren**-tay se-**sen**-ta ee **theen**-ko*
Yes, the AVE is the fastest one we've got. The second-class ticket costs 44 euros,
and the first-class one 65

Marisa **Turista no fumador, por favor. ¿Cuánto es?**
Tengo la tarjeta dorada, ¿hay algún descuento?
*too-**reess**-ta no foo-ma-**dor**, por fa-**bor**. kwan-to ess?*
***ten**-go la tar-**khe**-ta do-**ra**-da, aee al-**goon** dess-**kwen**-to?*
Non-smoking second class please. How much is it?
I've got a senior's railcard, is there a discount?

Assistant **Sí, en ese caso tiene un 50% de descuento.**
El total son 22 euros
*see, en **ess**-ay **ka**-so **tyen**-ay oon theen-**kwen**-ta por-**thyen**-to day dess-**kwen**-to. el tot-**al** son **bayn**-tay doss **eoo**-ross*
Yes, in this case you have a 50% discount.
The total is 22 euros

Marisa **Perfecto. Aquí tiene**
*per-**fek**-to. a-**kee tyen**-ay*
Fine. Here you are

Assistant **El tren sale por la vía dos, tiene el vagón 3, asiento 4A. Tenga el billete. Buen viaje**
*el tren **sa**-lay por la **bee**-a doss, **tyen**-ay el ba-**gon** tress, ass-**yen**-to **kwa**-tro a. ten-ga el bee-**yet**-ay. bwen **byakh**-ay*
The train leaves from track (platform) number two, coach 3, seat 4A

(on the platform)

Marisa **Oiga, el AVE para Madrid ¿cuál es? ¿Es ése?**
***oy**-ga, el **a**-bay **pa**-ra mad-**reed**, kwal ess? ess **ess**-ay?*
Excuse me, which one is the AVE to Madrid?
Is it this one?

Railwayman **No, no es ése. El de Madrid va con retraso, llegará dentro de algunos minutos**
*no, no ess **ess**-ay. el day mad-**reed** ba kon ret-**ra**-so, lyeg-a-**ra den**-tro day al-**goo**-noss mee-**noo**-toss*
No, it's not this one. The Madrid one is running late, it will arrive in a few minutes

Marisa **Pero es esta vía, ¿no?**
*pe-ro ess **ess**-ta **bee**-a, no?*
But it is this track (platform), isn't it?

Railwayman **Sí señora, es ésta**
*see sen-**yo**-ra, ess **ess**-ta*
Yes madam, it's this one

---

from the dialogue

un billete para ...
*oon bee-**yet**-ay **pa**-ra ...*
a ticket to ...

un billete de ida y vuelta
*oon bee-**yet**-ay day **ee**-da ee **bwel**-ta*
a return ticket

un billete de ida
*oon bee-**yet**-ay day **ee**-da*
a single ticket

¿a qué hora?
*a kay **o**-ra?*
what time?

más rápido
*ma **ra**-peed-o*
faster

sale por la vía ...
*sa-lay por la **bee**-a ...*
it leaves from platform number ...

tenga ...
***ten**-ga ...*
here's ...

ir con retraso
*eer kon ret-**ra**-so*
to be running late

¿cuál?
kwal?
which one?

éste
ess-tay
this one

ése
ess-ay
that one

dentro de algunos minutes
***den**-tro day al-**goo**-noss mee-**noo**-toss*
in a few minutes' time

Por and para again

Here's another way of telling por and para apart. Para gives the destination of the train, while por tells you its route or direction: el tren para Madrid sale por la vía dos y va por Zaragoza 'the train for Madrid leaves from platform two and goes via Zaragoza'. In the dialogue about the mugging, the policeman asked ¿por dónde huyó? 'which way did he run off?'; to use para there instead of por would imply some kind of insight into the mind of the robber, since we don't know his intended destination, only what his route was. > Prepositions RefZone 14

It's the one!

To give the time of the day in Spanish or 'the hour' la hora as it's called you need to make the verb agree with the number of hours. While in English we say it 'is' one o'clock or two o'clock, in Spanish es la una 'it's one o'clock' but son las dos/tres etc. > Time (telling the time) RefZone 4

Fast, faster, fastest

Superlatives ('the most' something-or-other) are just as straightforward as comparatives ('more' something-or-other). You just use más with the definite article: el AVE es el tren más rápido; es el más rápido que tenemos 'the AVE is the fastest train; it's the fastest we've got'. Madrid es una ciudad grande; es la más grande de España 'Madrid is a big city; it's the biggest in Spain'. Easy!

Fast talking

If you listen carefully to this dialogue on the CD you may notice that in the phrase más rapido 'faster, fastest' the s seems to disappear. This is what usually happens in normal rapid speech whenever an s is followed immediately by an r, a combination which Spanish speakers find difficult. It's certainly not wrong to pronounce the s, but little touches like this are a good way of making your Spanish sound more authentic.

This and that

Without the accent, este and ese (feminine esta and esa) are adjectives meaning 'this' and 'that': este tren 'this train', esa ciudad 'that city'. When you use the same words as pronouns you can add an accent to avoid ambiguity: éste/ésta 'this one', ése/ésa 'that one', plural: éstos/éstas and ésos/ésas. Contrast ¿qué tren? – este tren 'which train? – this train' with ¿cuál? – éste 'which one? – this one'.

Cutting corners

Most Spanish adjectives end in -o for masculine nouns and -a for feminine ones. So why buen viaje and not bueno? Well, while most adjectives come after the noun, some such as bueno 'good' and malo 'bad', can come before, and when they do they lose the -o in the masculine, so bueno becomes buen. El hotel es bueno: es un buen hotel. This also applies to alguno, as in algún postre 'some/any dessert' and its opposite ninguno/ningún 'no, not any', and the number adjectives primero and tercero 'first, third', as well as the number one itself, which is why the masculine indefinite article is un, as in un coche, instead of uno. > ADJECTIVES REFZONE 11

Getting your words in order

Grande is another adjective that sometimes loses its ending. It becomes gran when used before either a masculine or feminine noun. Note that it always follows the noun it describes when it means 'big' rather than 'great'. Thus, una ciudad grande 'a big city' but una gran ciudad 'a great city'.

now practise 23

> **travel vocabulary**

the film starts at ...
la película empieza a ...
la pel-ee-koo-la emp-yeth-a a ...

at one o'clock
a la una
a la oo-na

at two thirty
a las dos y media
a lass doss ee med-ya

at 1600 hours
a las dieciséis
a lass dyeth-ee-say-eess

at five to five
a las cinco menos cinco
a lass theen-ko men-oss theen-ko

at a quarter to six
a las seis menos cuarto
a lass seyss men-oss kwar-to

at twenty to seven
a las siete menos veinte
a lass syet-ay men-oss bayn-tay

at midnight
a medianoche
a med-ya-notch-ay

at midday
a mediodía
a med-yo-dee-a

at 22.48
a las veintidós cuarenta y ocho
a lass bayn-tee-doss kwa-ren-ta ee otch-o

Catching a bus

> **get to know ...**
>
> > saber and conocer
> > reflexives
> > tener que

Lydia **Oiga, ¿sabe si es éste el autobús que va al centro?**
*oy-ga, **sa**-bay see ess **ess**-tay el aoo-to-**booss** kay ba al **thent**-ro?*
Excuse me, do you know if this is the bus that goes to the city centre?

Marisa **Sí, eso es. Puede coger éste o el 10**
*see, **ess**-o ess. **pwed**-ay ko-**kher ess**-tay o el dyeth*
Yes, that's right. You can take this one or the number 10

Lydia **¿Pasan con frecuencia?**
***pa**-san kon fre-**kwenth**-ya?*
Do they go often?

Marisa **Sí, generalmente pasan cada diez minutos. El último pasó hace poco tiempo**
*see, khe-ne-ral-**men**-tay **pa**-san **ka**-da dyeth mee-**noo**-toss. el **ool**-tee-mo pa-**so** **ath**-ay **po**-ko **tyem**-po*
Yes, they generally go every ten minutes. The last one went by a short while ago

Lydia **¿Se puede comprar el billete en el autobús?**
*say **pwed**-ay komp-**rar** el bee-**yet**-ay en el aoo-to-**booss**?*
Can you buy the ticket on the bus?

Marisa **Sí, claro. Mire, por ahí viene el diez. Venga, ¡súbase!**
*see, **kla**-ro. **mee**-ray, por a-**ee byen**-ay el dyeth. **Ben**-ga, **soo**-ba-say!*
Yes, of course. Look, here comes the number 10. Come on, get on!

(on the bus)

Lydia **Hola, buenos días. Me da un billete, por favor?**
*o-la, **bwen**-oss **dee**-ass, may da oon bee-**yet**-ay, por fa-**bor**?*
Hello, good morning. Can I have a ticket please?

Driver **Son dos euros**
*son doss **eoo**-ross*
It's two euros

Lydia **Tenga. ¿Pasa por la Plaza Mayor?**
***ten**-ga. **pa**-sa por la **plath**-a ma-**yor**?*
Here you are. Do you go by the Plaza Mayor (main square)?

Driver **Sí, hay una parada justo a la entrada**
*see, aee **oo**-na pa-**ra**-da **khoo**-sto a la en-**tra**-da*
Yes, there's a stop just at the entrance

Lydia **¿Puede decirme cuándo tengo que bajarme? Es que no concozco la ciudad**
pwed**-ay de-**theer**-me **kwan**-do **ten**-go kay ba-**khar**-may? ess kay no ko-**noth**-ko la thyoo-**dad
Can you tell me when I need to get off? The thing is I don't know the city

Driver **Claro, no hay problema. Siéntese por aquí delante**
***kla**-ro, no aee prob-**lem**-a. **syen**-te-say por a-**kee** del-**an**-tay*
Sure, no problem. Sit here at the front

Knowing me, knowing you

Very often we find that one language 'has two words for the same thing', in other words there is a difference of meaning that doesn't exist in our own language - for example the way 'to ask' can be either preguntar (ask a question) or pedir (ask for something). Here's another of those things: 'to know' can be either saber or conocer depending on which sort of 'know' you mean. You can know a fact, be aware of something, know how to do something: that's saber. Or you can know a place or a person, be acquainted with it: conocer. No conozco la ciudad, ¿sabe? 'I don't know the town, you know?'

Not that again!

Yes, yet another demonstrative pronoun... Eso es is a common way of agreeing with someone, meaning 'that's it'. Unlike éste/ésta and ése/ésa, which mean 'this one', and 'that one', eso is non-gender-specific and doesn't refer to anything you could point to. It means 'that stuff, this business generally', as in 'that's the problem' or 'well, this is it!' So why doesn't it need an accent like the others do most of the time? Because there's no adjective corresponding to it, so there's nothing to distinguish it from.

Take that!

Here's another way of using the verb tener 'to have, hold' when handing something to someone. Tenga is the command form of tener corresponding to usted, literally 'have!' or 'hold!'

Lightning reflexes

In Spanish you 'get up onto' (subirse a) and 'get down from' (bajarse de) the bus, where in English we get 'on' and 'off'. The same with cars, even though there isn't really any up and down involved. A thowback to the early days of motoring where some real climbing was required! These are reflexive verbs: grammatically speaking, the action of the sentence is done by and to the same person or thing. In other words you 'raise yourself' or 'get yourself down'. As we've seen already, you need to glue the pronoun part onto the end of the verb when you make it into an instruction: isúbase! 'get on board!' siéntese por aquí delante 'sit here at the front'.

Gonna eat me a pie

Spanish sometimes uses reflexives where English doesn't. For example, we usually just 'wash' rather than 'wash ourselves'. There are many cases where a reflexive is optional, but is typically used in Spanish; for example, where you might 'buy' or 'eat' something, it's also very common to say comprar<u>se</u> algo or comer<u>se</u> algo - 'to buy yourself something', 'to have yourself something to eat', if you like.
> REFLEXIVE VERBS RefZone 33

---

did you know ...?

You can buy single tickets on the bus, but it's cheaper to by multiple tickets of 10 known as bónobus. These can be bought at kiosks and estancos 'tobacconists'. You must remember to validate the ticket in the machine next to the driver.

Got to be done!

Tener que is a useful phrase meaning 'to have to' and is followed by the infinitive. ¿Cuándo tengo que bajarme? 'when do I have to get off?' Tengo que salir 'I have to go out', tengo que hacer unas compras 'I have to do some shopping'. > TENER REFZONE 26

Watch your language!

Although European Spanish is very similar to Latin American Spanish there are a few words that you must watch out for. They mean something very different (and rude) so you don't want to provoke any shocked reactions. Coger is one of these words used in European Spanish to mean 'to catch' or 'to take' as in coger un taxi, coger un autobús, etc. In Latin American Spanish 'coger' means to engage in intercourse (but not of the spoken kind). So when in Mexico and South America, be careful what you use! You should use the verb tomar for catching public transport.

> saber and conocer

the bus station
la estación de autobuses
la ess-tath-yon day aoo-to-boos-ess

a bus stop
una parada de autobús
oo-na pa-ra-da day aoo-to-booss

to catch the bus
coger el autobús
ko-kher el aoo-to-boos

the timetable
el horario
el o-rar-yo

the coach
el autocar
el aoot-o-kar

the car ferry
el ferry
el fer-ree

the underground
el metro
el met-ro

the plane
el avión
el ab-yon

my flight
mi vuelo
mee bwel-o

departures
las salidas
lass sa-lee-dass

arrivals
las llegadas
lass lyeg-a-dass

to go by bike
ir en bici
eer en beeth-ee

now practise

25

An internet café

get to know ...

> que and qué
> internet vocabulary

Mónica **Sergio, ¿sabes dónde hay algún cibercafé por aquí cerca? Esta tarde tengo que mirar el correo y confirmar la asistencia a la reunión de la semana que viene**
serkh-yo, sa-bess don-day aee al-goon thee-ber-ka-fay por a-kee ther-ka? ess-ta tar-day ten-go kay mee-rar el ko-ray-o ee kon-feer-mar la a-sees-tenth-ya a la re-oon-yon day la se-ma-na kay byen-ay
Sergio, do you know where there is an internet café round here? This afternoon I need to look at my e-mail and to confirm that I'll be at next week's meeting

Sergio **Sí, hay uno en la calle de atrás de la plaza mayor. Está muy cerca**
see, aee oo-no en la ka-yay day a-trass day la plath-a ma-yor. ess-ta mwee ther-ka
Yes, there's one in the street behind the plaza mayor. It's very close

Mónica **¿Sabes cuánto cuesta conectarse?**
sa-bess kwan-to kwes-ta ko-nek-tar-say?
Do you know how much it costs to go online?

Sergio **Creo que son 5 euros la hora. Por cierto, no tengo tu email, ¿me lo puedes dar?**
kray-o kay son theen-ko eoo-ross la o-ra. por thyer-to, no ten-go too ee-mel. may lo pwed-ess dar?
I think it's five euros an hour. By the way, I haven't got your e-mail address, can you give it to me?

Mónica **Sí, es 'monica arroba internacional punto es'. ¿Cuál es el tuyo?**
see, ess mo-nee-ka ar-ro-ba een-ter-nath-yo-nal poon-to ess. kwal ess el too-yo?
Yes, it's monica@internacional.es. What's yours?

Sergio **alvarado arroba partida punto es. Es el email del trabajo porque aún no tengo uno personal. Me han hablado de un sitio para poder abrirme una cuenta de correo**
al-ba-ra-do ar-ro-ba par-tee-da poon-to ess. ess el ee-mel del tra-ba-kho por-kay a-oon no ten-go oo-no per-so-nal. may an ab-lad-o day oon seet-yo pa-ra po-der ab-reer-may oo-na kwen-ta day kor-ray-o
alvarado@partida.es. It's my work e-mail address, because I haven't got a home one yet. I've heard about a site I can open an e-mail account

Mónica **También tengo una página web. Es www.monicainternacional.es**
tamb-yen ten-go oo-na pakh-ee-na web. ess oo-bay-dob-lay oo-bay-dob-lay oo-bay-dob-lay mo-nee-ka een-ter-nath-yo-nal poon-to ess
I've also got a website. It's www.monicainternacional.es

The accent on question words

You already know about the accent on question words in simple questions such as, ¿dónde están? 'where are they?', ¿cuánto vale? 'how much is it?, ¿cómo estás? 'how are you? So it's probably no surprise that question words also have written accents in questions of the following sort: ¿sabes dónde hay algún cibercafé? 'do you know where there is an Internet café?; ¿sabes cuánto cuesta? do you know how much it costs? Remember that question words also have accents when they're given in reported questions and after expressions of doubt: me preguntó dónde había estado. 'he asked me where I'd been.' no sé qué hacer. 'I don't know what to do.'

What's what

Both ¿qué es ...? and ¿cuál es ...? can be used to ask what something is. But ¿qué es ...? is only used when you're asking for a definition of something. ¿Qué es el email? Es un sistema de comunicación. 'What's e-mail? It's a communication system.' So use ¿cuál es ...? in other contexts. ¿Cuál es tu email? 'What's your e-mail address?' ¿Cuál es tu número de teléfono? 'What's your telephone number?'

That's the ticket

Que is a very versatile word. It can mean 'that' when linking parts of a sentence as in creo que son 5 euros 'I think that it's 5 euros' and dijo que vendría 'he said that he'd come'. It can mean 'who', 'that' or 'which' when identifying the person or thing you're talking about: el chico que entró 'the boy who came in', el coche que compré 'the car that I bought'. And it's used in expressions like la semana que viene 'next week' (the week that's coming) and el año que viene 'next year' as well as in tener que 'to have to', tengo que mirar el email 'I must look at my e-mail' and hay que... 'one *or* you must...' as in hay que estudiar 'you have to study'.

Dialogue Zone | 65

from the dialogue

esta tarde
ess-ta *tar*-day
this afternoon

¿cúanto cuesta?
kwan-to *kwes*-ta?
how much does it cost?

conectarse
ko-nek-*tar*-say
to go online

cinco euros per hour
theen-ko *eoo*-ross la *o*-ra
5 euros la hora

por cierto
por *thyer*-to
by the way

el tuyo
el *too*-yo
yours

aún no
a-*oon* no
not yet

me han hablado de ...
muy un ub-*lad*-o day ...
I've heard about ...

26

It's not the same

Although in English we say 'it's one euro', 'it's five euros' and 'it's one hundred euros', in Spanish you have to make ser agree with what follows. Thus es un euro but son cinco euros and son cien euros. It's a similar distinction to the one you make when telling the time: es la una 'it's one o'clock' but son las tres 'it's three o'clock'. Compare too how the verb agrees when Spanish speakers identify themselves: soy yo 'it's me' and somos nosotros 'it's us'.

I want he should do it

More from that verb-form called the subjunctive, which typically deals with hypothetical or potential situations, such as desires and instructions. In English you can tell, ask, advise, or want 'someone to do something', but in Spanish you use the verb (tell, ask, advise, want or whatever) + que, followed by a verb in the subjunctive. For example, te aconsejo que visites mi sitio web 'I recommend you visit my website', dile que lo compre 'tell him to buy it', pídele que lo intente 'ask him to try', quiero que venga 'I want him to come'. The equivalent in English can often be expressed using the word 'should'. For example in ¿quieres que vaya contigo? 'do you want me to go with you?' is literally 'do you want that I should go with you?' The subjunctive verb endings are shown in the Reference Zone.

Where it's @

In these days of electronic communication, you often have to read out or understand the names for symbols like these. In Spanish use arroba for the 'at' symbol @, punto for the dot, barra for the slash and almohadilla for the hash symbol #. The code for Spain, .es, is pronounced as a word (ess) rather than two separate letters, just like '.com.' One little difference is that while we refer to 'the Internet' in English, the Spanish just call it Internet and not 'el Internet'.

Nuevo Message

a:	alopez@espasa.es
de:	monica@internacional.es
asunto:	reunion
cc:	
bcc:	

Estimados señores,

Les envío este mensaje para confirmar mi asistencia a la reunión del próximo día 13 de diciembre en Madrid a las 12:00.

Atentamente,
Mónica Clemente Díaz

Dear Sirs,

I am sending this message to confirm my attendance at the meeting of 13 December in Madrid at 12 o'clock.

Regards,
Mónica Clemente Díaz

Nuevo Message

a:	juan2@yahoo.es
de:	monica@internacional.es
asunto:	hola
cc:	
bcc:	

Hola Juan

¿Qué tal? Te mando esto porque estoy en un cibercafé y me sobran algunos minutos. Espero que todo te va bien. Hace años que no te veo. Tenemos que quedar en algún sitio para tomar algo, ¿no?

Un abrazo
Mónica

Hi Juan

How are you doing? I'm sending you this because I'm in an internet café and I have a few minutes spare. I hope everything's going OK with you. It's years since I've seen you. We must arrange to meet up somewhere for a drink, OK?

Cheers
Mónica

now practise

> **using possessives**

Booking a hotel

> **get to know ...**
>
> > dates
> > quisiera and quería
> > conditional tense

(on the phone)

Luis **Buenos días. Quisiera hacer una reserva para el cuatro al ocho de diciembre, cuatro noches**
*bwen-oss **dee**-ass. keess-**yer**-a ath-**er** oo-na ress-**er**-ba **pa**-ra el **kwa**-tro al **o**-tcho day deeth-**yem**-bray, **kwa**-tro **notch**-ess*
Good morning. I'd like to make a reservation for the 4th to the 8th of December, four nights

Receptionist **¿Habitación doble o individual?**
*a-bee-thath-**yon** **dob**-lay o een-dee-beed-**wal**?*
A double room or a single?

Luis **Doble, para dos adultos y un niño de siete años. ¿Sería posible poner una cama supletoria?**
*dob-lay, **pa**-ra doss a-**dool**-toss ee oon **neen**-yo day **syet**-ay **an**-yoss. se-**ree**-a po-**seeb**-lay po-**ner** oo-na **ka**-ma soop-let-**or**-ee-a?*
Double, for two adults and a child of seven years. Would it be possible to put in an extra bed?

Receptionist **Sí, no hay problema. El precio por noche son sesenta y cinco euros. ¿A qué nombre hago la reserva?**
*see, no aee prob-**lem**-a. el **preth**-yo por **notch**-ay son se-**sen**-ta ee **theen** ko **coo**-ross. a kay **nom**-bray **a**-go la ress-**er**-ba?*
Yes, no problem. The price per night is 65 euros. In what name shall I make the reservation?

Luis **Al mío, Luis Bernadetti**
*al **mee**-o, lweess ber-na-**det**-ee*
In my name, Luis Bernadetti

Receptionist **¿Cómo se escribe?**
*ko-mo say ess-**kree**-bay?*
How do you spell it?

Luis	**B, e, r, n, a, d, e, doble t, i**
	*bay, ay, **e**-ray, **en**-ay, a, day, ay, **dob**-lay tay, ee*
	B, e, r, n, a, d, e, double t, i
Receptionist	**¿Me dice un teléfono de contacto?**
	*may **dee**-thay oon te-**le**-fo-no day kon-**tak**-to?*
	Could you give me a contact phone number?
Luis	**Sí, nueve cincuenta y siete, doce, cero siete, noventa y siete**
	*see, **nweb**-ay theen-**kwen**-ta ee **syet**-ay, **doth**-ay, **thay**-ro **syet**-ay, no-**ben**-ta ee **syet**-ay*
	Yes, 957 12 07 97
Receptionist	**¿Y los datos de su tarjeta de crédito, con la fecha de caducidad?**
	*ee loss **da**-toss day soo tar-**khet**-a day **kre**-dee-to, kon la **fetch**-a day ka-dooth-ee-**dad**?*
	And your credit card details, with the expiry date?
Luis	**Enero de 2007. Mi número de tarjeta es ...**
	*e-**ne**-ro day doss meel **syet**-ay. mee **noo**-may-ro day tar-**khe**-ta ess ...*
	January 2007. My card number is ...

Two by two

Notice the way the phone number is laid out: 957 12 07 97. The Spanish don't give the digits one by one as you would in English, but tend to group them in pairs or threes: nueve cincuenta y siete, doce, cero siete, noventa y siete.

from the dialogue

hacer una reserva
*ath-**er** oo-na ress-**er**-ba*
to make a reservation

una habitación doble
*oo-na a-bee-tath-**yon dob**-lay*
a double room

una habitación individual
*oo-na a-bee-tath-**yon** een-dee-beed-**wal***
a single room

¿sería posible?
*se-**ree**-a po-**seeb**-lay?*
would it be possible?

supletorio
*soop-let-**or**-ee-o*
extra

por noche
*por **notch**-ay*
per night

¿cómo se escribe?
*ko-mo say ess-**kree**-bay?*
how do you spell it?

la fecha de caducidad
*la **fetch**-a day ka-dooth-ee-**dad***
the expiry date

enero de 2007
*e-**ne**-ro day dos meel **syet**-ay*
January 2007

Dating

In Spanish dates are not given using the 'ordinal' numbers, 'first', 'second', 'third' etc; you just talk about 'the eight of December' el ocho de diciembre, 'the sixteen of September' el diecisiete de septiembre, etc. Don't forget that months, like days of the week, don't have capital letters in Spanish.

If it wouldn't be too much trouble...

In much the same way as in English it feels more polite to say 'I'd like to' rather than 'I want to', in Spanish you can say quisiera or quería rather than quiero when asking for something: quisiera hacer una reserva 'I'd like to make a reservation'. But quiero is OK too.

That would be just dandy

Where in English you use 'would' for a hypothetical case 'I would do it if I had time', you need the 'conditional' tense: ¿sería possible poner una cama supletoria? 'would it be possible to put in an extra bed?'; estaría muy bien 'that would be very good'; me encantaría ir a Londres 'I'd love to go to London'; You'll notice it ends with -ía. As in English, the conditional can be used to make a request: me gustaría un café 'I'd like a coffee', nos gustaría visitar la catedral 'we'd like to visit the cathedral'. > Verbs RefZone 19.

Mine, all mine

Just as you can either say 'this train' (este tren) or 'this one' (éste), you can say 'my name' or 'mine'. In Spanish, as usual, there's a regular pattern. We've seen mi nombre and mi abuela for 'my...'. For 'mine' it's el mío for masculine nouns like nombre and la mía for feminine ones like abuela. That el can change to al, don't forget, when it follows a (a+el=al), so when Luis is asked in whose name the booking should be made, he replies 'in mine': al mío.

How much?!

Don't forget that to say how much something is, the choice of singular es or plural son depends on whether it's just one euro/pound/dollar, or more than one: son sesenta y cinco euros 'it's sixty-five euros'. So whereas in English we say 'the price *is* 65 euros' in Spanish the verb agrees with the '65 euros' (plural) and not the price (singular), el precio *son* 65 euros. If you think we have problems translating, remember it's the same for Spanish-speakers with English!

---

did you know ...?

The letter ñ is considered a separate letter in the Spanish alphabet. It follows n in alphabetical order. Ch and ll were also once considered separate letters with ch appearing after c and ll after l. This could be confusing when looking them up in a dictionary! Nowadays they are listed within the c and l entries and not treated separately.

In the name of the father and the mother

Spanish people don't have just one surname, they have two. They take their father's first surname as their first surname and their mother's first surname as their second. So if José Vigo Ruiz marries María Valle Nieto and they have two children, Pablo and Elena, Pablo and Elena's surnames will be Vigo Valle.

extra vocabulary

a family room
una habitación familiar
oo-na a-bee-tath-yon

with double bed
con cama de matrimonio
kon ka-ma day ma-tree-mon-yo

with twin beds
con dos camas
kon doss ka-mass

with bunk beds
con literas
kon lee-ter-ass

with bath
con baño
kon ban-yo

with shower
con ducha
kon doo-tcha

a cot
una cuna
oo-na koo-na

for one night
para una noche
pa-ra oo-na notch-ay

for Friday night
para la noche del viernes
pa-ra la notch-ay del byer-ness

now practise

> **spelling aloud and giving numbers**

Not feeling well

(on the phone)

Marta **¿Dígame?**
dee-ga-may?
Hello?

José **Hola Marta. Soy José. ¿Vas a venir al cine esta tarde?**
*o-la **mar**-ta. soy kho-**say**. bas a ben-**eer** al **theen**-ay **ess**-ta **tar**-day?*
Hello Marta. It's José. Are you going to come to the cinema this afternoon?

Marta **Creo que no porque no me encuentro bien**
***kray**-o kay no **por**-kay no may en-**kwen**-tro byen*
I don't think so, because I'm not well

José **¿Qué te pasa?**
*kay tay **pass**-a?*
What's the matter with you?

Marta **Me duele mucho la garganta y tengo ganas de vomitar. Creo que tengo fiebre**
*may **dwel**-ay **moo**-tcho la gar-**gan**-ta ee **ten**-go **ga**-nass day bom-ee-**tar**. **kray**-o kay **ten**-go **fyeb**-ray*
My throat is very painful and I feel sick. I think I've got a temperature

José **¿No habrás cogido la gripe?**
*no ab-**rass** ko-**khee**-do la **gree**-pay?*
Have you got flu, I wonder?

Marta **No sé, espero que no. Esta tarde voy a ir al médico**
*no say, ess-**pe**-ro kay no. **ess**-ta **tar**-day boy a eer al **med**-ee-ko*
I don't know, I hope not. This afternoon I'm going to the doctor's

José **¿Quieres que vaya contigo?**
***kyer**-ess kay **ba**-ya kon-**tee**-go?*
Do you want me to go with you?

Marta **No importa, gracias. Me va a acompañar Valle**
*no eem-**por**-ta, **grath**-yass. me ba a a-kom-pan-**yar ba**-yay*
It doesn't matter, thanks. Valle is going to come with me

José **Vale. Cuídate y no cojas frío. Te llamo mañana para ver como estás**
ba-lay. *kwee*-da-tay ee no *ko*-khass *free*-o. tay *ya*-mo man-*ya*-na *pa*-ra ber *ko*-mo ess-**tass**
OK. Look after yourself and don't catch cold. I'll phone you tomorrow to see how you are

Marta **Gracias y suerte esta tarde. Siento no poder ir**
grath-yass ee *swer*-tay **ess**-ta **tar**-day. **syen**-to no po-**der** eer
Thanks and good luck this afternoon. I'm sorry I can't come

José **No te preocupes. Que te mejores. Adiós**
no tay pray-o-**koo**-pess. kay tay me-**khor** ess. ud-**yoss**
Don't worry. Get well soon. Bye

from the dialogue

¿**dígame?**
dee-ga-may?
hello? *(on phone)*

creo que no
kray-o kay no
I don't think so

¿**qué te pasa?**
kay tay **pass**-a?
what's the matter with you?

me duele ...
may **dwel**-ay ...
my ... hurts

tener ganas de hacer algo
ten-**er ga**-nas day ath-**er al**-go
to want to do something

contigo
kon-**tee**-go
with you

¡**cuídate!**
kwee-da-tay!
look after yourself!

coger frío
ko-**khor free**-o
to catch cold

no te preocupes
no tay pray-o-**koo**-pess
don't worry

¡**que te mejores!**
kay tay mekh-**or**-ess!
get well soon!

Mañana

In Spanish there are a number of ways of saying what's going to happen. The future tense itself is only one of them, used especially for predictions: el martes sabremos los resultados 'we'll know the results on Tuesday'; mañana tendremos mucho trabajo 'we'll have a lot of work tomorrow'. As in English, you can state intentions using the verb for 'go' - ir - followed by a and another verb (in the infinitive): ¿vas a venir al partido de esta tarde? 'are you coming to the match this afternoon?'; me va a acompañar Valle 'Valle's coming with me'. Additionally, as in English, the present tense is often used to talk about planned events: te llamo mañana 'I'll call you tomorrow', esta tarde voy a Segovia 'I'm going to Segovia this afternoon'.

Got the urge

Tener ganas de hacer algo 'to feel like doing something' is a useful way of saying what you want to do, or in this case what your body wants to do! The word gana means an urge or desire, and tengo ganas de vomitar means 'I feel (like being) sick'.

Will it be flu?

There's another completely different use of the future tense here, to express a guess or supposition. We do this a bit in English ('that will be the taxi', 'I expect he'll be at the office now'). You can often translate this using 'must': ¡habrás cogido la gripe! 'you must have caught flu!' In this case, ¿no habrás cogido la gripe?, the use of no makes it seem more tentative: 'surely you can't have caught flu? could it be flu?'

I think so, I think not

How do you handle 'so' and 'not' in expressions of opinion? Easy: 'I think so' is creo que sí and 'I think not', or 'I don't think so' is creo que no - literally 'I think that yes' or 'I think that no'.

It pains me

When you like something, you say in Spanish that it 'pleases' you: me gusta España 'I like Spain', me encanta el sol 'I love the sun'. It's the same with less pleasant things: me duele la garganta 'my throat hurts', or literally 'my throat hurts me'. You can use this pattern to express all sorts of ailments, where we'd usually say 'ache' in English: me duele la cabeza 'I've got a headache' ('my head hurts me'), le duelen la pierna 'he's got a sore leg' ('his leg hurts him') and so on.

Not feeling myself

We've seen that Spanish often uses reflexive constructions, like me llamo Juan 'my name is Juan' and subirse al autobus 'to get on the bus'. This dialogue is full of them: no me encuentro bien 'I don't feel well' (literally 'I don't find myself well'); cuídate 'look after yourself'; no te preocupes 'don't worry (yourself)', and que te mejores 'get (yourself) better soon'. Note how the word for oneself, se, is attached to the end of the verb in the base or infinitive and imperative forms: subirse/¡súbase!, cuidarse/cuídate.
> REFLEXIVE VERBS REFZONE 33

Stuck with you

Here's another way a word can change when it joins with another, like a+el=al or de+el=del. 'With him/her' is con él/ella – no problem there - but when con comes up against the personal pronoun tú, you get contigo 'with you'. The others in this series are conmigo 'with me' and consigo 'with him (or himself)'.
> PRONOUNS REFZONE 18

Dos and don'ts

José tells Marta what to do and what not to do: cuídate y no cojas frío 'look after yourself and don't catch cold'. He's speaking to her as a friend, so he uses the tú form rather than usted. You can find the endings in the Reference Zone labelled 'imperative': cuidar to look after' something gives cuidas 'you look after' and in the reflexive icuídate! 'look after yourself!' If you're telling someone *not* to do something, though, you need a different form, the subjunctive: no te preocupes. We find the same form expressing a wish in que te mejores, 'may you get better', literally 'that you should get better' or 'let you be better'. To give orders to people you'd call usted or ustedes, as a waiter would do in a restaurant when telling customers where to sit, you use the subjunctive form to do the same job.

Heartfelt sorrow

'I'm sorry' is often expressed in Spanish as lo siento, literally 'I feel it'. You can also use this expression to specify what you're sorry about, using a verb after it: siento no poder ir 'I'm sorry to not be able to go', or siento tener que decir esto 'I'm sorry to have to say this'. To say you're sorry that *someone else* can't make it, you would need to use the subjunctive as outlined above: siento que no puedas ir 'I'm sorry *you* can't go'.

now practise   **31**

> **talking about the body**

I have stomachache
me duele el estómago
*may **dwel**-ay el ess-**tom**-a-go*

my back hurts
me duele la espalda
*may **dwel**-ay la ess-**pal**-da*

she has earache
le duelen los oídos
*lay **dwel**-an loss o-**ee**-doss*

he has toothache
le duelen las muelas
*lay **dwel**-en lass **mwel**-ass*

I feel dizzy
estoy mareado(a)
*ess-**toy** mar-ay-**a**-do(a)*

I'm pregnant
estoy embarazada
*ess-**toy** em-bar-ath-**a**-da*

he has high blood pressure
tiene la tensión alta
***tyen**-ay la ten-**syon al**-ta*

she's diabetic
es diabética
*ess dee-a-**bet**-ee-ka*

I've cut my finger
me he cortado el dedo
*may a kor-**tad**-o el **ded**-o*

he bumped his head
se golpeó la cabeza
*say gol-pay-**o** la ka-**beth**-a*

she had a fall
se cayó
*say ka-**yo***

A visit to London

get to know ...

> geographical names
> informal Spanish
> hacer in expressions of time

Maite **¡Hombre! ¿Qué tal? Hace años que no te veo**
om-bray! kay tal? **ath**-ay **an**-yoss kay no tay **bay**-o
Hey! How are you doing? It's been years since I've seen you

Antonio **Bien, tía. Es que he estado en Londres estudiando inglés**
byen, **tee**-a. ess kay ay ess-**ta**-do en **lon**-dress ess-too-dee-**an**-do een-**gless**
I'm fine, sweetheart. Actually I've been in London studying English

Maite **¡Qué suerte tienes! Me encantaría visitar Londres. Me parece una ciudad muy emocionante**
kay **swer**-tay **tyen**-ess! may en-kan-ta-**ree**-a bee-see-**tar lon**-dress. may pa-**reth**-ay **oo**-na thyoo-**dad** mwee e-moth-yon-**an**-tay
You're so lucky! I'd love to go to London. I think it's a very exciting city

Antonio **Sí, a mí también. Es estupendo, me lo he pasado muy bien**
see, a mee tamb-**yen**. ess ess-too-**pen**-do, may lo ay pa-**sa**-do mwee byen
Me too. It's great, I had a really good time

Maite **Será muy caro, ¿verdad?**
se-**ra** mwee **ka**-ro, ber-**dad**?
I suppose it must be very expensive?

Antonio **Ya lo creo. Pero conozco a una familia muy maja allí, y me han alojado en su casa. Así ahorras un montón de pasta, claro**
ya lo **kray**-o. **pe**-ro ko-**noth**-ko a **oo**-na fa-**meel**-ya mwee **ma**-kha a-**yee**, ee may an a-lo-**kha**-do en soo **ka**-sa. a-**see** a-**orr**-ass oon mon-**ton** day **pas**-ta, **kla**-ro
I should say so. But I know a very nice family there, and they put me up. That way you save loads of dosh, obviously

Maite **Pues qué bien, hijo. So, you have learned English good, ¿no?**
pwess kay byen, **ee**-kho. ...
Well, great stuff mate. ...

Antonio **¿Qué?**
kay?
You what?

Long since

Hace años que no te veo, 'it's years since last I saw you' or 'I haven't seen you for years'. Remember that, in this Spanish construction, the tenses work very differently from their English equivalents. A literal translation would be: 'it makes years that I don't see you' (present tense). In the same way, a Spanish speaker could say hace mucho tiempo que viven aquí 'they've lived here for ages'. Other similar constructions work in the same way, as we've seen before.

Aunts and uncles? Sons and daughters?

Bien, tía, says the boy to the girl; pues qué bien, hijo, she says to him. In informal Spanish, you'll often hear people who aren't related addressing one another as tío 'uncle' and tía 'aunt', or hijo 'son' hija 'daughter'. It's just like saying 'mate' or 'love' in English. You can also refer to someone as un tío 'a bloke, a guy', or in the case of a woman, una tía.

from the dialogue

¡hombre!
om-bray!
hey!

hace años que ...
ath-ay an-yoss kay ...
it's been years since ...

¡qué suerte!
kay swer-tay!
what luck!

me encantaría ...
may en-kan-ta-ree-a ...
I'd love to ...

me parece ...
may pa-reth-ay ...
it seems to me ... /I think ...

¡ya lo creo!
ya lo kray-o!
I should say so!

pues
pwess
well

¡qué bien!
kay byen!
great stuff!

It'll cost you!

As we saw earlier, people often use the future in Spanish to express a guess or supposition: ¿no habrás cogido la gripe? 'could you have caught flu? Here it is again: será muy caro 'it must be very expensive', 'I expect it will be very expensive'.

Am I right or am I right?

In English we often use phrases like 'isn't it?', 'don't you?', 'is he?', to check that the person we're talking to agrees. In Spanish people use ¿verdad? (literally 'truth?') and ¿no? in the same way: es caro, ¿verdad? or es caro, ¿no? 'it's expensive, isn't it?; ¿no te gusta, ¿verdad? 'you don't like it, do you?' When the previous statement is negative (no te gusta) you use ¿verdad? rather than ¿no?

Slangtastic

The informal style of this dialogue contains various colloquial expressions you may come across if you spend any time around Spanish people. Apart from the use of tía and hijo, we have majo for 'nice, great' (una familia muy maja) and un montón de pasta 'masses of money', terms you wouldn't use in a formal letter. See the vocabulary panel for some more informal expressions.

How useful!

It's that versatile little word again, que/qué. You can follow it with almost anything – ¡qué suerte! 'what luck! how lucky!', ¡qué calor! 'it's so hot!' – or an adverb – ¡qué bien! 'how nice! great stuff!' – or an adjective – ¡qué bonito! 'how pretty!'

Changing names

Spanish has its own names, not just for countries, but for many major cities, from Londres (London) to Edimburgo (Edinburgh) to Bruselas (Brussels) to Hamburgo (Hamburg).

Getting personal

Did you notice that Antonio said 'I know a family' conozco a una familia? You might be wondering where the a came from. An interesting aspect of Spanish grammar is what is called the 'personal a'. It is used when the direct object of a verb (in this case, a family) is a person. So 'they love their children' is quieren mucho a sus hijos. As it doesn't appear in English, so it's easy to miss it out. However, it's not used with tener, so 'I have two children' is tengo dos hijos and not tengo a dos hijos as you might expect.

What's your opinion?

An expression used to give opinions is me parece 'it seems to me'. Here Maite thinks that London is a very exciting city me parece una ciudad muy emocionante. So you could say me parece muy caro for 'it seems (to me) very expensive'. If you want to add a verb you insert que – me parece que es muy caro 'I think that it is very expensive'. Note that if you use it in a negative way, the following verb has to be in the subjunctive no me parece que sea muy caro. Me parce que ... is a very common way of saying 'I think that ...'.

extra vocabulary

great
estupendo
ess-too-pen-do

cool
genial
khen-yal

a bloke
un tío
oon tee-o

the cops
los polis
loss pol-eess

work
el curro
el koor-ro

no way!
ini hablar!
nee ab-lar!

I just don't believe it!
ino me lo creo!
no may lo kray-o!

nonsense!
iqué va!
kay ba!

what a drag!
iqué pesado!
kay pess-a-do!

now practise **33**

> **weather terms**

Word Zone (English–Spanish)

A

a(n) un(a)

able: *to be able* poder

above arriba ; por encima

to accept aceptar

accident el accidente

address la dirección

adult el/la adulto(a)

afraid: *to be afraid of* tener miedo de

after después

afternoon la tarde
this afternoon esta tarde
in the afternoon por la tarde

again otra vez

age la edad

ago: *a week ago* hace una
semanaairport el aeropuerto

all todo(a)/todos(as)

allergic to alérgico(a) a

to allow permitir

all right *(agreed)* de acuerdo
(OK) vale

almost casi

alone solo(a)

already ya

also también

always siempre

a.m. de la mañana

America Norteamérica

American norteamericano(a)

amount el total

and y

angry enfadado(a)

anniversary el aniversario

another otro(a)
another beer, please otra cerveza,
por favor

answer la respuesta

to answer responder

apartment el apartamento

apple la manzana

appointment *(meeting)* la cita

(dentist, hairdresser) la hora

apricot el albaricoque

April abril

arm el brazo

to arrange organizar

arrival la llegada

to arrive llegar

art gallery la galería de arte

artist el/la artista

to ask *(question)* preguntar
(to ask for something) pedir

at a ; en
at home en casa
at 8 o'clock a las ocho
at once ahora mismo
at night por la noche

August agosto

aunt la tía

Australia Australia

Australian australiano(a)

autumn el otoño

available disponible

average medio(a)

to avoid *(issue)* evitar

B

baby el bebé

bad *(weather, news)* mal/malo(a)
(fruit and vegetables) podrido(a)

bag la bolsa

baggage el equipaje

baker's la panadería

bald *(person)* calvo(a)
(tyre) gastado(a)

ball *(large: football, etc)* el balón
(small: golf, tennis, etc) la pelota

banana el plátano

bank el banco

bank account la cuenta bancaria

bar el bar

basement el sótano

bath el baño
to have a bath bañarse

bathroom el cuarto de baño

battery *(radio, camera, etc)* la pila
(in car) la batería

to be estar ; ser

beach la playa

beard la barba

beautiful hermoso(a)

because porque

to become hacerse

bed la cama

bedroom el dormitorio

beer la cerveza

before antes de

to begin empezar

behind detrás de

to belong to pertenecer a
(club) ser miembro de

below debajo ; por debajo

beside *(next to)* al lado de
beside the bank al lado del banco

best el/la mejor

better mejor
better than mejor que

between entre

bicycle la bicicleta
by bicycle en bicicleta

big grande
bigger than mayor que

bill la factura
(in restaurant) la cuenta

bird el pájaro

biro el boli

birth el nacimiento

birth certificate la partida de
nacimiento

birthday el cumpleaños
happy birthday! ¡feliz cumpleaños!
my birthday is on... mi
cumpleaños es el...

bit: *a bit of* un poco de

to bite morder
(insect) picar

black negro(a)

blind *(person)* ciego(a)

blond (person) rubio(a)

blood la sangre

blouse la blusa

blue azul

boat (large) el barco
  (small) la barca

body el cuerpo

book el libro

to book reservar

booking la reserva

boring aburrido(a)

born: I was born in... nací en...

to borrow pedir prestado

both ambos(as)

bottle la botella

box la caja

boy el chico

boyfriend el novio

bread el pan

to break romper

breakfast el desayuno

to bring traer

Britain Gran Bretaña

British británico(a)

broken roto(a)

brother el hermano

brother-in-law el cuñado

brown marrón

brush el cepillo

to burn quemar

bus el autobús

bus stop la parada de autobús

business el negocio
  on business de negocios

busy ocupado(a)

but pero

butcher's la carnicería

butter la mantequilla

to buy comprar

by (via) por
  (beside) al lado de
  by air en avión
  by car en coche
  by train en tren

C

café el café
  internet café el cibercafé

cake (big) la tarta
  (little) el pastel

call (telephone) la llamada

to call (phone) llamar por teléfono

camera la cámara

to camp acampar

campsite el camping

to can (to be able) poder

can la lata

can opener el abrelatas

Canada (el) Canadá

Canadian canadiense

to cancel anular ; cancelar

capital (city) la capital

car el coche

car park el aparcamiento

carafe la jarra

caravan la caravana

card (greetings, business) la tarjeta
  playing cards las cartas

careful cuidadoso(a)
  be careful! ¡ten cuidado!

carpet (rug) la alfombra

carriage (railway) el vagón

to carry llevar

carton la caja

case (suitcase) la maleta

to cash (cheque) cobrar

cash desk la caja

castle el castillo

cat el gato

to catch (bus, train, etc) coger

cathedral la catedral

CD el CD

CD player el lector de CD

cellar la bodega

centimetre el centímetro

centre el centro

certain (sure) seguro(a)

chair la silla

change el cambio
  (small coins) el suelto
  (money returned) la vuelta

to change cambiar
  (clothes) cambiarse

charge (fee) el precio

to charge cobrar

cheap barato(a)

cheaper más barato(a)

to check revisar ; comprobar

cheese el queso

chemist's la farmacia

cheque el cheque

chicken el pollo

child (boy) el niño
  (girl) la niña

children (infants) los niños
  for children para niños

chips las patatas fritas

chocolate el chocolate

chocolates los bombones

to choose escoger

Christmas la Navidad
  Merry Christmas! ¡Feliz Navidad!

Christmas card la tarjeta de
  Navidad

Christmas Eve la Nochebuena

church la iglesia

cigarette el cigarrillo

cigarette lighter el mechero

cinema el cine

city la ciudad

clean limpio(a)

to clean limpiar

clear claro(a)

client el/la cliente

clock el reloj

close by muy cerca

to close cerrar

closed (shop, etc) cerrado(a)

clothes la ropa

coach (bus) el autocar

coat el abrigo

code el código

coffee el café
  black coffee el café solo
  white coffee el café con leche

cold frío(a)
  I'm cold tengo frío
  it's cold hace frío

cold (illness) el resfriado
  I have a cold estoy resfriado(a)

to collect recoger

colour el color

comb el peine

to come venir
  (to arrive) llegar

to come back volver

to come in entrar
  come in! ¡pase!

company (firm) la empresa

to complain reclamarcompulsory
  obligatorio(a)

computer program el programa
  de ordenador

concert el concierto

concert hall la sala de conciertos

concession el descuento

conference el congreso

to confirm confirmar

confirmation la confirmación

congratulations! ¡enhorabuena!

to consult consultar

to continue continuar

to cook cocinar

cooker la cocina

cool fresco(a)

copy (duplicate) la copia
  (of book) el ejemplar

to copy copiar

corkscrew el sacacorchos

corner la esquina

corridor el pasillo

cost (price) el precio

to cost costar
  how much does it cost? ¿cuánto
  cuesta?

country (not town) el campo
  (nation) el país

couple (2 people) la pareja
  a couple of... un par de ...

cousin el/la primo(a)

crash (car) el accidente

cream (lotion) la crema
  (on milk) la nata

credit card la tarjeta de crédito

crisps las patatas fritas

to cross (road) cruzar

crossing (sea) la travesía

crossroads el cruce

cruise el crucero

to cry (weep) llorar

cup la taza

cupboard el armario

curtain la cortina

custom (tradition) la costumbre

customer el/la cliente

customs (control) la aduana

to cycle ir en bicicleta

D

daily (each day) cada día ; diario

to dance bailar

dangerous peligroso(a)

dark oscuro(a)
  after dark por la noche

date la fecha

daughter la hija

daughter-in-law la cuñada

day el día
  every day todos los días

dead muerto(a)

deaf sordo(a)

dear (on letter) querido(a)
  (expensive) caro(a)

December diciembre

deep profundo(a)

delay el retraso

delicatessen la charcutería

delicious delicioso(a)

dentist el/la dentista

department store los grandes
  almacenes

departures las salidasdesk (in hotel,
  airport) el mostrador

dessert el postre

detour el desvío

to develop (photos) revelar

to dial marcar

dialling code el prefijo

diapers los pañales

diary la agenda

dictionary el diccionario

to die morir

diesel el diesel ; el gasóleo

diet la dieta
  I'm on a diet estoy a dieta

digital camera la cámara digital

digital radio la radio digital

to dilute diluir

dining room el comedor

dinner (evening meal) la cena
  to have dinner cenar

directions: to ask for directions
  preguntar el camino

directory (phone) la guía telefónica

dirty sucio(a)

disabled minusválido(a)

to disappear desaparecer

to discover descubrir

district el barrio

to disturb molestar

divorced divorciado(a)

to do hacer

doctor el/la médico(a)

documents los documentos

dog el perro

domestic (flight) nacional

door la puerta

doorbell el timbre

down: to go down bajar

to download descargar

downstairs abajo

drawing el dibujo

dress el vestido

to dress (to get dressed) vestirse

drink la bebida

to drink beber

to drive conducir

driver el/la conductor(a)

drug la droga
  (medicine) la medicina

dry seco(a)

to dry secar

during durante

duvet el edredón nórdico

E

each cada

ear (outside) la oreja
  (inside) el oído

early temprano

to earn ganar

earrings los pendientes

earth la tierra

east el este

Easter la Pascua ; la Semana Santa

easy fácil

to eat comer

egg el huevo

either... or... o... o...elevator el ascensor

e-mail el email ; el correo electrónico
to e-mail s.o. mandar un email a alguien

e-mail address el email

empty vacío(a)

end el fin

engaged *(to marry)* prometido(a)
(toilet, phone) ocupado(a)

engine el motor

England Inglaterra

English inglés/inglesa
(language) el inglés

Englishman/-woman el inglés/ la inglesa

to enjoy *(to like)* gustar
I enjoy dancing me gusta bailar
enjoy your meal! ¡qué aproveche!

to enjoy oneself divertirse

enough bastante
that's enough ya basta

to enter entrar en

entrance la entrada

error el error

to escape escapar

euro el euroEuropean Union la Unión Europea

even *(not odd)* par

evening la tarde
this evening esta tarde
in the evening por la tarde

evening meal la cena

every cada

everyone todo el mundo ; todos

everything todo

examination el examen

example: *for example* por ejemplo

excellent excelente

exchange el cambio

to exchange cambiar

exchange rate el tipo de cambio

exciting emocionante

excuse: *excuse me!* perdón

exhibition la exposición

exit la salida

expenses los gastos

expensive caro(a)

to expire *(ticket, etc)* caducar

to explain explicar

express *(train)* el expreso

extra *(in addition)* de más
(more) extra ; adicional

eye el ojo

F

face la cara

to faint desmayarse

fair *(hair)* rubio(a)
(just) justo(a)

fall *(autumn)* el otoño

to fall caer ; caerse
he/she has fallen se ha caído

family la familia

famous famoso(a)

fan *(electric)* el ventilador
(hand-held) el abanico
(football, etc) el/la hincha
(jazz, etc) el/la aficionado(a)

far lejos
Is it far? ¿esta lejos?

fast rápido(a)
too fast demasiado rápido

to fasten *(seatbelt, etc)* abrocharse

fat *(plump)* gordo(a)
(in food, on person) la grasa

father el padre

father-in-law el suegro

fault *(defect)* el defecto
it's not my fault no tengo la culpa

favourite favorito(a) ; preferido(a)

to fax mandar por fax

fax el faxFebruary febrero

to feed dar de comer

to feel sentir
I don't feel well no me siento bien

feet los pies

female mujer

ferry el ferry ; el transbordador

festival el festival

to fetch *(to bring)* traer
(to go and get) ir a buscar

few pocos(as)
a few algunos(as)

fiancé(e) el/la novio(a)to fill llenar
(form) rellenar
fill it up, please! (car) lleno, por favor

film *(at cinema)* la película
(for camera) el carrete

to find encontrar

fine *(to be paid)* la multa

finger el dedo

to finish acabar

fire *(flames)* el fuego
(blaze) el incendio

fire brigade los bomberos

firm *(company)* la empresa

first primero(a)

first class de primera clase

first name el nombre de pila

fish *(food)* el pescado
(alive) el pez

to fish pescar

fishmonger's la pescadería

to fit *(clothes)* quedar bien

to fix arreglar

fizzy con gas

flag la bandera

flat *(apartment)* el piso

flat llano(a)
(battery) descargado(a)

flat tyre la rueda pinchada

flavour el sabor

flight el vuelo

flood la inundación

floor *(of building)* el piso
(of room) el suelo
which floor? ¿qué piso?
the ground floor la planta baja
on the first floor en el primer piso

flower la flor

flu la gripe

to fly volar

fog la niebla

to follow seguir

foot el pie
on foot a pie

football el fútbol

for para ; por
 for me para mí

forbidden prohibido(a)

foreign extranjero(a)

foreigner el/la extranjero(a)

forever para siempre

to forget olvidar

fork *(for eating)* el tenedor
 (in road) la bifurcación

form *(document)* el impreso

forward adelante

France Francia

free *(not occupied)* libre
 (costing nothing) gratis

French fries las patatas fritas

fresh fresco(a)

Friday el viernes

fridge el frigorífico

fried frito(a)

from de ; desde
 from Scotland de Escocia

front la parte delantera
 in front of delante de

to fry freír

full lleno(a)
 (occupied) ocupado(a)

fun la diversión

funny *(amusing)* divertido(a)

furniture los muebles

G

game el juego

garage el garaje
 (for repairs) el taller
 (for petrol) la gasolinera

garden el jardín

gas el gas

gay *(person)* gay

gear la marcha
 neutral el punto muerto
 reverse la marcha atrás

generous generoso(a)

gents *(toilet)* los servicios
 de caballeros

German alemán/alemana
 (language) el alemán

Germany Alemania

to get *(to obtain)* conseguir
 (to receive) recibir
 (to bring) traer

to get in *(vehicle)* subir (al)

to get out *(of vehicle)* bajarse de

gift el regalo

girl la chica

girlfriend la novia

to give dar

to give back devolver

glass *(for drinking)* el vaso
 (substance) el cristal

glasses *(spectacles)* las gafas

to go ir
 to go home irse a casa

to go back volver

to go in entrar (en)

to go out salir

God Dios

gold el oro

good bueno(a)

goodbye adiós

good day buenos días

good evening buenas tardes
 (when dark) buenas noches

good night buenas noches

grandchild el/la nieto(a)

grandfather el abuelo

grandmother la abuela

grandparents los abuelos

great *(big)* grande
 (wonderful) estupendo(a)

Great Britain Gran Bretaña

green verde

grocer's la tienda de alimentación

ground el suelo

ground floor la planta baja

guesthouse la pensión

guide *(tour guide)* el/la guía

guidebook la guía turística

H

hair el pelo

half medio(a)
 half an hour media hora

half-price a mitad de precio

ham el jamón

(cooked) el jamón de York
 (cured) el jamón serrano

hand la mano

handbag el bolso

hand luggage el equipaje de mano

hand-made hecho(a) a mano

handicapped minusválido(a)

handkerchief el pañuelo

to happen pasar

happy feliz
 happy birthday! ¡feliz cumpleaños!

harbour el puerto

hard duro(a)
 (difficult) difícil

hard disk el disco duro

hardware shop la ferretería

hat el sombrero

to have tener

to have to tener que

head la cabeza

headache el dolor de cabeza
 I have a headache me duele
 la cabeza

headlights los faros

headphones los auriculares

healthy sano(a)

to hear oír

heart el corazón

heart attack el infarto

heavy pesado(a)

heel *(of foot)* el talón
 (of shoe) el tacón

height la altura

hello hola
 (on phone) ¿diga?

help! ¡socorro!

to help ayudar
 can you help me? ¿puede
 ayudarme?

here aquí
 here is... aquí tiene...

to hide *(something)* esconder
 (oneself) esconderse

high alto(a)

hill la colina

hire *(bike, boat, etc)* el alquiler

to hire alquilar

to hit pegar

holiday las vacaciones
(public) la fiesta
on holiday de vacaciones

home la casa
at home en casa

honeymoon la luna de miel

to hope esperar
I hope so/not espero que sí/no

horse el caballo

horse riding la equitación

hospital el hospital

hot caliente
I'm hot tengo calor
it's hot (weather) hace calor

hotel el hotel

hour la hora

house la casa

housewife/husband la/el ama(o)
de casa

house wine el vino de la casa

how *(in what way)* cómo
how much? ¿cuánto?
how many? ¿cuántos?

hungry: *to be hungry* tener hambre

hurry: *I'm in a hurry* tengo prisa

to hurt *(injure)* hacer daño
my back hurts me duele la espalda
that hurts eso duele

husband el marido

I

ice el hielo
with/without ice con/sin hielo

icecream el helado

identity card el carné de identidad

if si

ill enfermo(a)

illness la enfermedad

immediately en seguida

important importante

impossible imposible

to improve mejorar

in dentro de ; en
in 10 minutes dentro de diez
minutos
in London en Londres

in front of delante de

included incluido(a)

indicator *(in car)* el intermitente

indigestion la indigestión

indoors dentro

information la información

to injure herir

inside dentro de

instead of en lugar de

insurance el seguro

to intend to pensar

interesting interesante

internet el/la Internet
internet café el cibercafé

interval *(theatre, etc)* el descanso

interview la entrevista

into en
into town al centro

to introduce to presentar a

invitation la invitación

to invite invitar

Ireland Irlanda

Irish irlandés/irlandesa

iron *(for clothes)* la plancha
(metal) el hierro

ironmonger's la ferretería

island la isla

it lo/la

Italian italiano(a)
(language) el italiano

Italy Italia

J

jacket la chaqueta

jam *(food)* la mermelada

jammed *(stuck)* atascado(a)

January enero

jeans los vaqueros

job el empleo

to join *(club, etc)* hacerse socio de

to join in participar en

to joke bromear

journalist el/la periodista

journey el viaje

jug la jarra

juice el zumo

July julio

June junio

just: *just two* sólo dos
I've just arrived acabo de llegar

K

to keep *(to retain)* guardar

key la llave

kilo(gram) el kilo(gramo)

kind *(person)* amable

kind *(sort)* la clase
what kind? ¿qué clase?

to kiss besar

kitchen la cocina

knee la rodilla

knife el cuchillo

to knock *(on door)* llamar

to knock down *(car)* atropellar

to knock over *(vase, glass)* tirar

to know *(have knowledge of)* saber
(person, place) conocer

to know how to saber
to know how to swim saber nadar

L

ladder la escalera (de mano)

lady la señora

lake el lago

land el terreno

language el idioma ; la lengua

laptop el ordenador portátil

large grande

last último(a)
last night anoche
last week la semana pasada
last time la última vez

late tarde
the train is late el tren viene con
retraso
sorry I'm late siento llegar tarde

later más tarde

to laugh reírse

to learn aprender

leather el cuero

to leave *(a place)* irse de
(leave behind) dejar
when does the train leave?
¿a qué hora sale el tren?

left: *on/to the left* a la izquierda

left-luggage *(office)* la consigna

leg la pierna

lemon el limón

lemonade la gaseosa

to lend prestar

lens *(phototgraphic)* el objetivo
  (contact lens) la lentilla

less menos
  less than menos de que

to let *(to allow)* permitir
  (to hire out) alquilar

letter la carta
  (of alphabet) la letra

letterbox el buzón

library la biblioteca

licence el permiso
  (driving) el carné de conducir

to lie down acostarse

lift *(elevator)* el ascensor
  can you give me a lift? ¿me lleva?

light *(not heavy)* ligero(a)

light la luz
  have you a light? ¿tiene fuego?

like *(similar to)* como

to like gustar
  I like coffee me gusta el café

lips los labios

to listen to escuchar

litre el litro

litter *(rubbish)* la basura

little pequeño(a)
  a little... un poco...

to live vivir
  he lives in a flat vive en un piso

living room el salón

to lock cerrar con llave

locker *(luggage)* la consigna

long largo(a)
  for a long time (por) mucho
  tiempo

to look after cuidar

to look at mirar

to look for buscar

lorry el camión

to lose perder

lost perdido(a)
  I'm lost me he perdido

lot: *a lot of* mucho

loud *(sound, voice)* fuerte
  (volume) alto(a)

lounge el salón

love el amor

to love *(person)* querer

lovely precioso(a)

low bajo(a)

luck la suerte

luggage el equipaje

lunch la comida

M

mad loco(a)

magazine la revista

maiden name el apellido de soltera

mail el correo
  by mail por correo

main principal

make *(brand)* la marca

to make hacer

man el hombre

to manage *(be in charge of)* dirigir

manager el/la gerente

many muchos(as)

map *(of region, country)* el mapa
  (of town) el plano

March marzo

mark *(stain)* la mancha

market el mercado

married casado(a)
  I'm married estoy casado(a)

to marry casarse con

match *(game)* el partido

matches las cerillas

to matter importar
  what's the matter? ¿qué pasa?

May mayo

meal la comida

to mean querer decir

meat la carne

to meet *(by chance)* encontrarse con
  (by arrangement) ver

meeting la reunión

member *(of club, etc)* el/la socio(a)

memory card la tarjeta de memoria

men los hombres

to mend arreglar

menu la carta
  set menu el menú del día

message el mensaje

metre el metro

metro *(underground)* el metro

midday las doce del mediodía

middle el medio

midnight la medianoche

mile la milla

milk la leche

mind: *do you mind if...?* ¿le importa
  que...?

mineral water el agua mineral

minute el minuto

mirror el espejo

to miss *(train, etc)* perder

Miss la señorita

mistake el error

to mix mezclar

mobile (phone) el (teléfono) móvil

Monday el lunes

money el dinero
  I've no money no tengo dinero

month el mes
  this month este mes
  last month el mes pasado
  next month el mes que viene

more más
  more than más que
  more wine más vino

morning la mañana
  in the morning por la mañana
  this morning esta mañana

most: *most of* la mayor parte de ;
  la mayoría de

mother la madre

mother-in-law la suegra

motor el motor

motorbike la moto

motorway la autopista

mountain la montaña

mouse *(animal, computer)* el ratón

mouth la boca

to move mover

Mr el señor (Sr.)

Mrs la señora (Sra.)

Ms la señora (Sra.)

much mucho(a)
  too much demasiado(a)

museum el museo

music la música
must (to have to) deber
my mi

N

nail (fingernail) la uña
(metal) el clavo
name el nombre
my name is... me llamo...
nappies los pañales
nationality la nacionalidad
navy blue azul marino
near to cerca de
is it near? ¿está cerca?
necessary necesario(a)
neck el cuello
to need necesitar
needle la aguj
neighbour el/la vecino(a)
nephew el sobrino
net la red
never nunca
I never drink wine nunca bebo vino
new nuevo(a)
news (TV, radio, etc) las noticias
newsagent's la tienda de prensa
newspaper el periódico
New Year el Año Nuevo
New Year's Eve la Nochevieja
New Zealand Nueva Zelanda
next próximo(a)
next to al lado de
next week la próxima semana
nice (person) simpático(a)
(place, holiday) bonito(a)
niece la sobrina
night la noche
at night por la noche
last night anoche
per night por noche
tonight esta noche
nightdress el camisón
no no
no smoking prohibido fumar
(without) sin
no ice sin hielo
nobody nadie
noise el ruido

none ninguno(a)
non-smoking no fumador
north el norte
Northern Ireland Irlanda del Norte
nose la nariz
nothing nada
nothing else nada más
notice (sign) el anuncio
(warning) el aviso
November noviembre
now ahora
nowhere en ninguna parte
number el número
nurse la/el enfermera(o)
nuts (to eat) los frutos secos

O

to obtain obtener
occupation (work) la profesión
ocean el océano
October octubre
odd (strange) raro(a)
(not even) impar
of de
a glass of wine un vaso de vino
made of... hecho(a) de...
off (light, etc) apagado(a)
(rotten) pasado(a)
office la oficina
often a menudo
how often? ¿cada cuánto?
oil el aceite
OK ¡vale!
old viejo(a)
I'm ... years old tengo ... años
olive la aceituna
olive oil el aceite de oliva
on (light, TV, engine) encendido(a)
on sobre ; encima
on the table sobre la mesa
on time a la hora
once una vez
at once en seguida
only sólo
open abierto(a)
to open abrir
opposite (to) enfrente (de)
or o

orange (fruit) la naranja
(colour) naranja
orange juice el zumo de naranja
order: out of order averiado(a)
organic biológico(a) ; ecológico(a)
to organize organizar
other: the other one el/la otro(a)
out (light) apagado(a)
he's (gone) out ha salido
outside: it's outside está fuera
oven el horno
over (on top of) (por) encima de
to overtake (in car) adelantar
to owe deber
I owe you... le debo...
owner el/la propietario(a)

P

to pack (luggage) hacer las maletas
packet el paquete
page la página
paid pagado(a)
I've paid he pagado
pain el dolor
painful doloroso(a)
painkiller el analgésico
to paint pintar
panties las bragas
pants (men's underwear)
los calzoncillos
paper el papel
parents los padres
park el parque
to park aparcar
partner (business) el/la socio(a)
(boy/girlfriend) el/la compañero(a)
party (group) el grupo
(celebration) la fiesta
(political) el partido
pass (mountain) el puerto
(train) el abono
(bus) el bonobús
passenger el/la pasajero(a)
passport el pasaporte
path el camino
patient (in hospital) el/la paciente
to pay pagar
payphone el teléfono público

peach el melocotón

pear la pera

pen el bolígrafo ; el boli

pencil el lápiz

pensioner el/la jubilado(a)

people la gente

per por
per day al día
per hour por hora
per person por persona
50 km per hour 50 km por hora

perfect perfecto(a)

perhaps quizá(s)

permit el permiso

person la persona

pet el animal doméstico

petrol la gasolina
unleaded petrol la gasolina sin plomo

petrol station la gasolinera

pharmacy la farmacia

phone el teléfono
(mobile) el móvil
(hands free) el teléfono 'manos libres'
by phone por teléfono

to phone llamar por teléfono

phonebook la guía (telefónica)

phonebox la cabina (telefónica)

photograph la fotografía
to take a photograph hacer una fotografía

to pick *(choose)* elegir
(pluck) coger

picnic el picnic
to have a picnic ir de picnic

picture *(painting)* el cuadro
(photo) la foto

piece el trozo

pill la píldora
to be on the pill tomar la píldora

pink rosa

pity: *what a pity* ¡qué pena!

place el lugar

plain *(yoghurt)* natural

plan *(of town)* el plano

plane *(airplane)* el avión

platform el andén
which platform? ¿qué andén?

to play *(games)* jugar

pleasant agradable

please por favor

pleased contento(a)
pleased to meet you encantado(a) de conocerle(la)

pocket el bolsillo

poison el veneno

police *(force)* la policía

policeman/woman el/la policía

pool la piscina

poor pobre

popular popular

port *(seaport)* el puerto
(wine) el oporto

possible posible

post: *by post* por correo

postbox el buzón

postcard la postal

post office la oficina de Correos

to postpone aplazar

potato la patata

to pour echar ; servir

powder el polvo

to prefer preferir

to prepare preparar

present *(gift)* el regalo

pretty bonito(a)

price el precio

prime minister el/la primer(a) ministro(a)

print *(photo)* la copia

to print imprimir

private privado(a)

prize el premio

problem el problema

professor el/la catedrático(a)

programme *(TV, radio)* el programa

prohibited prohibido(a)

to promise prometer

public público(a)

public holiday la fiesta (oficial)

to pull tirar

pullover el jersey

puncture el pinchazo

purple morado(a)

purpose el propósito
on purpose a propósito

purse el monedero

to push empujar

pushchair la sillita de paseo

to put *(place)* poner

pyjamas el pijama

Pyrenees los Pirineos

Q

quality la calidad

quantity la cantidad

to quarrel discutir ; pelearse

queen la reina

question la pregunta

to queue hacer cola

quick rápido(a)

quiet *(place)* tranquilo(a)

quite bastante
quite expensive bastante caro

R

radio la radio

railway station la estación de tren

rain la lluvia

to rain: *it's raining* está lloviendo

raincoat el impermeable

rare *(unique)* excepcional
(steak) poco hecho(a)

raspberry la frambuesa

rate *(price)* la tarifa

razor la maquinilla de afeitar

to read leer

ready listo(a)
to get ready prepararse

real verdadero(a)

receipt el recibo

reception desk la recepción

to recognize reconocer

to recommend recomendar

to recover *(from illness)* recuperarse

red rojo(a)

reduction el descuento

to refuse negarse

region la región
relationship la relación
to remain (stay) quedarse
to remember acordarse (de)
   I don't remember no me acuerdo
to remove quitar
rent el alquiler
to rent alquilar
rental el alquiler
repair la reparación
to repeat repetir
reservation la reserva
to reserve reservar
rest (repose) el descanso
   (remainder) el resto
to rest descansar
restaurant el restaurante
retired jubilado(a)
to return (to go back) volver
   (to give back something) devolver
return (ticket) de ida y vuelta
reverse gear la marcha atrás
rice el arroz
rich (person) rico(a)
   (food) pesado(a)
to ride a horse montar a caballo
right (correct) correcto(a)
   to be right tener razón
right: on/to the right a la derecha
to ring (bell, to phone) llamar
ring el anillo
ripe maduro(a)
river el río
road la carretera
roast asado(a)
roof el tejado
room (in house, hotel) la habitación
   (space) sitio
rose la rosa
round (shape) redondo(a)
roundabout (traffic) la rotonda
royal real
rubber (material) la goma
   (eraser) la goma de borrar
rubbish la basura
rucksack la mochila
to run correr

S

sad triste
safe seguro(a)
safe (for valuables) la caja fuerte
salary el sueldo
salt la sal
same mismo(a)
sand la arena
sandals las sandalias
sandwich el bocadillo ; el sándwich
Saturday el sábado
sauce la salsa
to save (life) salvar
   (money) ahorrar
to say decir
scarf (woollen) la bufanda
   (headscarf) el pañuelo
school la escuela ; el colegio
scissors las tijeras
Scotland Escocia
Scottish escocés/escocesa
screen (computer, TV) la pantalla
screwdriver el destornillador
sea el mar
seaside la playa
season (of year) la estación
   (holiday) la temporada
   in season del tiempo
seat (chair) la silla
   (in bus, train) el asiento
seatbelt el cinturón de seguridad
second segundo(a)
second (time) el segundo
second-hand de segunda mano
secretary el/la secretario(a)
to see ver
to sell vender
to send enviar
senior citizen el/la jubilado(a)
separated (couple) separado(a)
September septiembre
serious (accident, etc) grave
to serve servir
service station la estación de
   servicio
set menu el menú del día
several varios(as)

to share compartir ; dividir
to shave afeitarse
sheet (bed) la sábana
shelf el estante
shirt la camisa
shoe el zapato
shop la tienda
to shop hacer las compras
shop assistant el/la dependiente(a)
shopping centre el centro
   comercial
short corto(a)
to shout gritar
show (theatrical) el espectáculo
to show enseñar
shower (bath) la ducha
   (rain) el chubasco
   to take a shower ducharse
to shut cerrar
sick (ill) enfermo(a)
   I feel sick tengo ganas de vomitar
side el lado
sign la señal
to sign firmar
signature la firma
silk la seda
silver la plata
similar to parecido(a) a
since desde ; puesto que
   since 1974 desde 1974
   since you're not Spanish puesto
   que no es español(a)
to sing cantar
single (unmarried) soltero(a)
   (bed, room) individual
sister la hermana
sister-in-law la cuñada
to sit sentarse
   sit down, please siéntese, por
   favor
size (clothes) la talla
   (shoes) el número
to ski esquiar
skin la piel
skirt la falda
sky el cielo
to sleep dormir
slice (of bread) la rebanada

(of ham) la loncha
slide (photo) la diapositiva
slow lento(a)
slowly despacio
small pequeño(a)
smaller than más pequeño(a) que
smell el olor
to smile sonreir
to smoke fumar
smoke el humo
smooth liso(a)
snack el tentempié
snack bar la cafetería
to sneeze estornudar
to snore roncar
snow la nieve
to snow nevar
  it's snowing está nevando
soap el jabón
socks los calcetines
some algunos(as)
someone alguien
something algo
sometimes a veces
son el hijo
son-in-law el yerno
soon pronto
  as soon as possible lo antes posible
sore throat el dolor de garganta
sorry: sorry! ¡perdón!
  I'm sorry! ¡lo siento!
sort el tipo
south el sur
Spain España
Spaniard el/la español(a)
Spanish español(a)
sparkling espumoso(a)
to speak hablar
special especial
spell: how is it spelt? ¿cómo se escribe?
to spend (money) gastar
spoon la cuchara
spring (season) la primavera
square (in town) la plaza
stairs las escaleras

stamp (postage) el sello
to stand estar de pie
star la estrella
to start (car) poner en marcha
station la estación
stay la estancia
  enjoy your stay! ¡que lo pase bien!
to stay (remain) quedarse
to steal robar
stepfather el padrastro
stepmother la madrastra
still (not fizzy) sin gas
stomach el estómago
to stop parar
store (shop) la tienda
storey el piso
storm la tormenta
  (at sea) el temporal
story la historia
straightaway inmediatamente
straight on todo recto
straw (for drinking) la pajita
strawberry la fresa
street la calle
street map el plano de la ciudad
strong fuerte
stuck: it's stuck está atascado(a)
student el/la estudiante
stuffed relleno(a)
stung picado(a)
stupid tonto(a)
subway (train) el metro
  (passage) el paso subterráneo
sugar el azúcar
suit (men's and women's) el traje
suitcase la maleta
summer el verano
sun el sol
Sunday el domingo
sunny: it's sunny hace sol
supermarket el supermercado
surname el apellido
surprise la sorpresa
surrounded by rodeado(a) de
to survive sobrevivir
sweet (dessert) el dulce

sweets los caramelos
to swim nadar
swimming pool la piscina
swimsuit el bañador
switch el interruptor
to switch off apagar
to switch on encender

T

table la mesa
to take (medicine, etc) tomar
  how long does it take? ¿cuánto tiempo se tarda?
to talk to hablar con
tall alto(a)
tank (petrol) el depósito
  (fish) la pecera
tap el grifo
to taste probar
taxi el taxi
tea el té
teapot la tetera
to teach enseñar
teacher el/la profesor(a)
team el equipo
teeth los dientes
telephone el teléfono
to telephone llamar por teléfono
television la televisión
to tell decir
temperature la temperatura
  to have a temperature tener fiebre
temporary provisional
tent la tienda de campaña
terrace la terraza
to test (try out) probar
to text mandar un mensaje de texto a
text message el mensaje de texto
to thank agradecer
thank you gracias
that ese/esa
  (more remote) aquel/aquella
  that one ése/ésa/eso
  (more remote) aquél/aquélla/aquello
the el/la/los/las

theatre el teatro

theft el robo

their su/sus

these estos/estas
these ones éstos/éstas

thin *(person)* delgado(a)

thing la cosa
my things mis cosas

to think pensar
(to be of opinion) creer

thirsty: *I'm thirsty* tengo sed

this este/esta/esto
this one éste/ésta

those esos/esas
(more remote) aquellos/aquellas
those ones ésos/ésas
(more remote) aquéllos/aquéllas

throat la garganta

through por

Thursday el jueves

ticket *(bus, train, etc)* el billete
(entrance fee) la entrada
a single ticket un billete de ida
a return ticket un billete de ida
y vuelta

tie la corbata

till *(until)* hasta
till 2 o'clock hasta las 2

time el tiempo
(clock) la hora
what time is it? ¿qué hora es?

timetable el horario

tin *(can)* la lata

tip la propina

tired cansado(a)

to a
to London a Londres

tobacconist's el estanco

today hoy

together juntos(as)

toilet los aseos ; los servicios

tomato el tomate

tomorrow mañana
tomorrow morning mañana por
la mañana
tomorrow afternoon mañana por
la tarde
tomorrow evening mañana por
la tarde/noche

tonight esta noche

too *(also)* también
too big demasiado grande
too small demasiado pequeño(a)

tooth el diente

toothbrush el cepillo de dientes

toothpaste la pasta de dientes

top: *the top floor* el último piso

torch *(flashlight)* la linterna

total *(amount)* el total

tour *(trip)* el viaje
(of museum, etc) la visita

tour guide el/la guía turístico(a)

tourist el/la turista

to tow remolcar

towel la toalla

tower la torre

town la ciudad

town centre el centro de la ciudad

town plan el plano de la ciudad

toy el juguete

traditional tradicional

traffic el tráfico

traffic jam el atasco

traffic lights el semáforo

train el tren
by train en tren

trainers las zapatillas de deporte

to translate traducir

to travel viajar

travel agent's la agencia de viajes

tree el árbol

trip la excursión

trolley *(luggage, shopping)* el carrito

trousers los pantalones

truck el camión

true verdadero(a)

truth la verdad

to try *(attempt)* probar

to try on *(clothes)* probarse

Tuesday el martes

tunnel el túnel

to turn girar

to turn around girar

to turn off *(light, etc)* apagar
(tap) cerrar

to turn on *(light, etc)* encender
(tap) abrir

tyre el neumático

U

umbrella el paraguas
(sunshade) la sombrilla

uncle el tío

uncomfortable incómodo(a)

under debajo de

underground *(metro)* el metro

underpants los calzoncillos

to understand entender

underwear la ropa interior

to undress desvestirse

United Kingdom el Reino Unido

United States Estados Unidos

university la universidad

to unlock abrir (con llave)

unpleasant desagradable

up: *to get up* levantarse

upstairs arriba

USA EE.UU.

to use usar

useful útil

usually por lo general

V

vacancy *(in hotel)* la habitación libre

vacant libre

vacation las vacaciones

van la furgoneta

VAT el IVA

vegan vegetariano(a) estricto(a)

vegetables las verduras

vegetarian vegetariano(a)

very muy

vet el/la veterinario(a)

via por

to video *(from TV)* grabar (en vídeo)

village el pueblo

to visit visitar

visitor el/la visitante

W

to wait for esperar

waiter/waitress el/la camarero(a)

to wake up despertarse

Wales Gales

walk un paseo
to go for a walk dar un paseo

to walk andar

wall (inside) la pared
   (outside) el muro

wallet la cartera

to want querer

war la guerra

ward (hospital) la sala

warm caliente
   it's warm (weather) hace calor

to wash (oneself) lavar(se)

to watch (look at) mirar

watch el reloj

water el agua

way (manner) la manera
   (route) el camino

way in (entrance) la entrada

way out (exit) la salida

to wear llevar

weather el tiempo

web (internet) el/la Internet

website la página web

wedding la boda

Wednesday el miércoles

week la semana
   last week la semana pasada
   next week la semana que viene
   per week por semana
   this week esta semana

weekday el día laborable

weekend el fin de semana

to weigh pesar

welcome! ¡bienvenido(a)!

well bien

Welsh galés/galesa
   (language) el galés

west el oeste

wet mojado(a)
   (weather) lluvioso(a)

what? ¿qué?

wheel la rueda

wheelchair la silla de ruedas

when? ¿cuándo?

where? ¿dónde?

which? ¿cuál?

while: in a while dentro de un rato

white blanco(a)

who? ¿quién?

whole entero(a)

whose? ¿de quién?

why? ¿por qué?

wide ancho(a)

widow la viuda

widower el viudo

wife la mujer

wild salvaje

to win ganar

wind el viento

window la ventana
   (shop) el escaparate
   (in car, train) la ventanilla

windscreen el parabrisas

windy: it's windy hace viento

wine el vino
   red wine el (vino) tinto
   white wine el vino blanco

winter el invierno

with con

without sin

woman la mujer

wonderful maravilloso(a)

wood (material) la madera
   (forest) el bosque

word la palabra

work el trabajo

to work (person) trabajar
   (machine, car) funcionar

world el mundo

worse peor

worth: it's worth... vale...

to wrap (parcel) envolver

to write escribir

wrong: what's wrong ¿qué pasa?

X

X-ray la radiografía

Y

year el año
   this year este año
   next year el año que viene
   last year el año pasado

yellow amarillo(a)

yes sí

yesterday ayer

yet: not yet todavía no

young joven

youth hostel el albergue juvenil

Z

zip la cremallera

zoo el zoo

Word Zone (Spanish–English)

A

a to ; at
  a la estación to the station
  a las 4 at 4 o'clock
  a 30 kilómetros 30 km away
abajo below ; downstairs
abierto(a) open
abogado(a) *m/f* lawyer
abono *m* season ticket
abrebotellas *m* bottle opener
abrelatas *m* tin-opener
abrigo *m* coat
abril *m* April
abrir to open ; to turn on *(tap)*
abuela *f* grandmother
abuelo *m* grandfather
aburrido(a) boring
acabar to finish
acampar to camp
aceite *m* oil
aceituna *f* olive
accra *f* pavement ; sidewalk
acompañar to accompany
aconsejar to advise
actor *m* actor
actriz *f* actress
acuerdo *m* agreement
adelantar to overtake *(in car)*
adiós goodbye ; bye
admitir to accept ; to permit
adolescente *m/f* teenager
aduana *f* customs
advertir to warn
aeropuerto *m* airport
afeitarse to shave
aficionado(a) *m/f* fan
afilado(a) sharp *(razor, knife)*
agencia *f* agency
  agencia de viajes travel agency
agenda *f* diary
agitar to shake *(bottle)*
agosto *m* August
agotado(a) sold out ; out of stock

agradable pleasant
agua *f* water
agudo(a) sharp ; pointed
aguja *f* needle ; hand *(on watch)*
agujero *m* hole
ahora now
ahorrar to save *(money)*
aire *m* air
ajo *m* garlic
albaricoque *m* apricot
albergue *m* hostel
alcanzar to reach ; to get
alemán(mana) German
Alemania *f* Germany
alérgico(a) a allergic to
alfombra *f* carpet ; rug
algo something
algodón *m* cotton
alguien someone
alguno(a) some ; any
algunos(as) some ; a few
alimentación *f* grocer's ; food
allí there *(over there)*
almacén *m* store ; warehouse
  grandes almacenes department
  stores
almohada *f* pillow
almuerzo *m* lunch
alojamiento *m* accommodation
alquilar to rent ; to hire
alrededor about ; around
alto(a) high ; tall
altura *f* altitude ; height
alubia *f* bean
amable pleasant ; kind
amarillo(a) yellow ; amber
ambos(as) both
ambulatorio *m* health centre
amigo(a) *m/f* friend
amor *m* love
ananá(s) *m* pineapple
andar to walk
andén *m* platform

anillo *m* ring
animal *m* animal
  animal doméstico pet
aniversario *m* anniversary
  aniversario de boda wedding
  anniversary
año *m* year
  Año Nuevo New Year
antes (de) before
anticonceptivo *m* contraceptive
anular to cancel
anuncio *m* advertisement ; notice
apagar to switch off ; to turn off
aparcamiento *m* car park
aparcar to park
apartamento *m* flat ; apartment
apellido *m* surname
apertura *f* opening
aprender to learn
aquí here
árbitro *m* referee
árbol *m* tree
arena *f* sand
armario *m* wardrobe ; cupboard
arrancar to start
arreglar to fix ; to mend
arriba upstairs ; above
arroz *m* rice
artesanía *f* crafts
asado(a) roast
asegurar to insure
aseos *mpl* toilets
asiento *m* seat
aspiradora *f* vacuum cleaner
ataque *m* fit *(seizure)*
atascado(a) jammed *(stuck)*
atasco *m* hold-up *(traffic jam)*
aterrizar to land
atrás behind
atropellar to knock down *(car)*
aumentar to increase
auricular *m* receiver *(phone)*
autostop *m* hitch-hiking

autobús *m* bus

autocar *m* coach (bus)

automático(a) automatic

autopista *f* motorway

autor(a) *m/f* author

autoservicio *m* self-service

Av./Avda. *abbrev. for* avenida

avenida *f* avenue

avería *f* breakdown (car)

averiado(a) out of order

avión *m* airplane ; aeroplane

aviso *m* notice ; warning

ayer yesterday

ayudar to help

ayuntamiento *m* town/city hall

azafata *f* air hostess ; stewardess

azúcar *m* sugar

azul blue

B

bailar to dance

bajar to go down

bajarse (del) to get off (bus, etc)

bajo(a) low ; short ; soft (sound)

balneario *m* spa

balón *m* ball

bañador *m* swimming costume

bañarse to go swimming ; to have a bath

banco *m* bank ; bench

bandera *f* flag

baño *m* bath ; bathroom

barato(a) cheap

barba *f* beard

barca *f* small boat

barco *m* ship ; boat

barra *f* bar ; counter ; bread stick

barrio *m* district ; suburb

bastante enough ; quite

basura *f* rubbish ; litter

batería *f* battery (in car)

batido *m* milkshake

bautizo *m* christening

to be ser ; estar

bebé *m* baby

beber to drink

bebida *f* drink

besar to kiss

beso *m* kiss

betún *m* shoe polish

biblioteca *f* library

bici *f* bicycle

bicicleta *f* bicycle

bien well

bienvenido(a) welcome

bigote *m* moustache

billete *m* ticket
    billete de ida single ticket
    billete de ida y vuelta return ticket

billetera *f* wallet

blanco(a) white

blusa *f* blouse

boca *f* mouth

bocadillo *m* sandwich

boda *f* wedding

bodega *f* wine cellar ; restaurant

bolígrafo *m* biro ; pen

bollo *m* roll ; bun

bolsa *f* bag ; stock exchange

bolsillo *m* pocket

bolso *m* handbag

bomba *f* pump (bike, etc) ; bomb

bomberos *mpl* fire brigade

bombilla *f* light bulb

bombonería *f* confectioner's

bonito(a) pretty ; nice-looking

bono *m* voucher

bonobús *m* bus pass

botella *f* bottle

bragas *fpl* knickers

brazo *m* arm

británico(a) British

bromear to joke

bronceador *m* suntan lotion

broncearse to tan

bueno(a) good ; fine

buscador *m* search engine

buscar to look for

buzón *m* postbox ; letterbox

C

caballeros *mpl* gents

caballo *m* horse
    montar a caballo to go riding

cabello *m* hair

cabeza *f* head

cable *m* wire ; cable

cacahuete *m* peanut

cada every ; each
    cada día daily (each day)

caducado(a) out-of-date

caducar to expire (ticket, passport)

caer(se) to fall

café *m* café ; coffee
    café con leche white coffee
    café solo black coffee

caja *f* cashdesk ; box

cajero(a) *m/f* teller ; cashier
    cajero automático cash dispenser ; auto-teller

calcetines *mpl* socks

calefacción *f* heating

calendario *m* calendar

calentar to heat up (milk, etc)

caliente hot

calle *f* street ; fairway (golf)

calvo(a) bald

calzoncillos *mpl* underpants

cama *f* bed

cámara *f* camera ; inner tube

camarera *f* waitress ; chambermaid

camarero *m* barman ; waiter

cambiar to change ; to exchange
    cambiarse to get changed

cambio *m* change ; gear

caminar to walk

camino *m* path ; road ; route

camión *m* lorry

camisa *f* shirt

camiseta *f* t-shirt ; vest

camisón *m* nightdress

campana *f* bell

campo *m* countryside ; field ; pitch

caña *f* cane ; rod
    caña (de cerveza) glass of beer

cancelar to cancel

canción *f* song

candado *m* padlock

cansado(a) tired

cantante *m/f* singer

cantar to sing

cantidad *f* quantity

cara *f* face

cárcel *f* prison

cargar to load

carne *f* meat

carné de conducir *m* driving licence

carné de identidad *m* identity card

carnicería *f* butcher's

caro(a) dear ; expensive

carrete *m* film *(for camera)*

carretera *f* road

carrito *m* trolley

carta *f* letter ; playing card ; menu

cartera *f* wallet ; briefcase

cartero(a) *m/f* postman/woman

cartón *m* cardboard

casa *f* house ; home ; household

casado(a) married

casarse (con) to marry

casco *m* helmet

casi almost

caso: en caso de in case of

castellano(a) Spanish ; Castilian

castillo *m* castle

catalán/catalana Catalonian

causa *f* cause
    a causa de because of

ceder to give way

celo *m* Sellotape®

cementerio *m* cemetery

cena *f* dinner ; supper

cenar to have dinner

cenicero *m* ashtray

céntimo *m* euro cent

centro *m* centre

cepillo *m* brush

cerca (de) near ; close to

cerillas *fpl* matches

cero *m* zero

cerrado(a) closed

cerradura *f* lock

certificado(a) registered

cervecería *f* pub

cerveza *f* beer ; lager

chaqueta *f* jacket

charcutería *f* delicatessen

cheque *m* cheque

chica *f* girl

chico *m* boy

chico(a) small

chiringuito *m* beach bar ; stall

chocar to crash *(car)*

chocolate *m* chocolate ;
    hot chocolate

chófer *m* chauffeur ; driver

chubasco *m* shower *(rain)*

ciego(a) blind

cielo *m* sky ; heaven

cien hundred

cifra *f* number ; figure

cigarrillo *m* cigarette

cigarro *m* cigar ; cigarette

cima *f* top ; peak

cine *m* cinema

cinta *f* tape ; ribbon

cintura *f* waist

cinturón *m* belt

circulación *f* traffic

circular to drive ; to circulate

cita *f* appointment

ciudad *f* city ; town

claro(a) light *(colour)* ; clear

clase *f* class ; type ; lesson
    clase preferente club/business
    class

cliente *m/f* customer ; client

climatizado(a) air-conditioned

cobrar to charge ; to cash

cobro *m* payment

cocer to cook ; to boil

coche *m* car ; coach *(on train)*

cocido(a) cooked ; boiled

cocina *f* kitchen ; cooker ; cuisine

cocinar to cook

código *m* code

coger to catch ; to get ;
    to pick up *(phone)*

cola *f* glue ; queue ; tail

colchón *m* mattress

colegio *m* school

colgar to hang up

colina *f* hill

color *m* colour

comedor *m* dining room

comer to eat

comestibles *mpl* groceries

comida *f* food ; meal

comisaría *f* police station

como as ; like ; since

¿cómo? how? ; pardon?

cómodo(a) comfortable

compañero(a) *m/f* colleague ;
    partner

compañía *f* company

completo(a) full ; no vacancies

comportarse to behave

comprar to buy

comprender to understand

con with

concierto *m* concert

concurrido(a) busy ; crowded

conducir to drive

conductor(a) *m/f* driver

confirmar to confirm

confitería *f* cake shop

congelado(a) frozen

conjunto *m* group *(music)*

conocer to know ; to be
    acquainted with

conseguir to obtain

conservar to keep

consigna *f* left-luggage office

construir to build

consultorio *m* doctor's surgery

consumir to eat ; to use

contagioso(a) infectious

contener to hold *(to contain)*

contento(a) pleased

contestador automático *m*
    answerphone

contra against

copa *f* glass ; goblet

copia *f* copy ; print *(photo)*

corazón *m* heart

correo *m* mail
    correo electrónico e-mail

Correos *m* post office

correr to run

corrida de toros *f* bullfight

cortado(a) blocked *(road)*

cortar to cut

corto(a) short

cosa *f* thing

cosecha *f* harvest ; vintage *(wine)*

costar to cost
costumbre f custom (tradition)
creer to think ; to believe
crema f cream (lotion)
cremallera f zip
cruce m junction ; crossroads
crucero m cruise
crudo(a) raw
cruzar to cross
c/u (cada uno) each (one)
cuadro m picture ; painting
¿cuál? which?
¿cuándo? when?
¿cuánto? how much?
¿cuántos? how many?
Cuaresma f Lent
cuarto m room
cubierto m cover charge
cubierto(a) covered ; indoor
cubrir to cover
cuchara f spoon
cucharilla f teaspoon
cuchillo m knife
cuenta f bill ; account
cuero m leather
cuerpo m body
cuidado m care
cumpleaños m birthday
cuñado(a) m/f brother/sister-in-
   law

D

daños mpl damage
dar to give
datos mpl data ; information
dcha. abbrev. for derecha
de of ; from
de acuerdo all right (agreed)
debajo (de) under ; underneath
deber to owe ; to have to
debido(a) due
decir to tell ; to say
declarar to declare
dedo m finger
   dedo del pie toe
dejar to let ; to leave
delante de in front of

delgado(a) thin ; slim
delito m crime
demasiado too much
dentadura postiza f dentures
dentífrico m toothpaste
dentista m/f dentist
dentro (de) inside
dependiente(a) m/f sales assistant
deporte m sport
derecha f right(-hand side)
derecho m right ; law
desabrochar to unfasten
desaparecer to disappear
desayuno m breakfast
descansar to rest
descanso m rest ; interval
descargado(a) flat (battery)
descargar to download
describir to describe
descubrir to discover
descuento m discount
desde since ; from
desear to want
desempleado(a) unemployed
deseo m wish ; desire
despacho m office
despacio slowly ; quietly
despertador m alarm (clock)
despertarse to wake up
después after ; afterward(s)
destornillador m screwdriver
desvestirse to get undressed
desvío m detour ; diversion
detrás (de) behind
devolver to give/put back
día m day
diario(a) daily
dibujo m drawing
diccionario m dictionary
diciembre m December
diente m tooth
dieta f diet
¿diga? hello (on phone)
dinero m money
Dios m God
dirección f direction ; address
directo(a) direct (train, etc)

director(a) m/f director ; manager
dirigir to manage
disco m record ; disk
   disco duro hard disk
discrecional optional
discutir to quarrel ; to argue
diseño m design ; drawing
disponible available
distinto(a) different
divertido(a) funny (amusing)
divertirse to enjoy oneself
divisa f foreign currency
divorciado(a) divorced
doblado(a) folded ; dubbed (film)
doble double
dolor m ache ; pain
doloroso(a) painful
domicilio m home address
domingo m Sunday
¿dónde? where?
dormir to sleep
dormitorio m bedroom
droga f drug
ducha f shower
ducharse to take a shower
dueño(a) m/f owner
dulce sweet
dulce m dessert ; sweet
duro(a) hard ; tough

E

echar to pour ; to throw ; to post
ecológico(a) organic
edad f age (of person)
edificio m building
edredón (nórdico) m duvet ; quilt
EE.UU. USA
ejemplar m copy (of book)
el the
electricidad f electricity
elegir to choose
embajada f embassy
embarazada pregnant
embarque m boarding
emitido por issued by
emocionante exciting
empezar to begin

empresa *f* firm ; company

empujar to push

en in ; into ; on

encantado(a) pleased to meet you!

encargado(a) *m/f* person in charge

encendedor *m* (cigarette) lighter

encender to switch on ; to light

enchufar to plug in

enchufe *m* plug ; point ; socket

encontrar to find

encontrarse con to meet *(by chance)*

enero *m* January

enfadado(a) angry

enfermo(a) ill

enfrente (de) opposite

¡enhorabuena! congratulations!

enlace *m* connection *(train, etc)*

ensalada *f* salad

enseñar to show ; to teach

entender to understand

entero(a) whole

entierro *m* funeral

entrada *f* entrance ; admission

entrar to go in ; to enter

entre among ; between

entregar to deliver

entrevista *f* interview

enviar to send

envolver to wrap

equipaje *m* luggage ; baggage

equipo *m* team ; equipment

escalera *f* stairs ; ladder

escanear to scan

escáner *m* scan

escapar to escape

escaparate *m* shop window

escocés(cesa) Scottish

Escocia *f* Scotland

escoger to choose

esconder to hide

escribir to write

escrito: por escrito in writing

escuchar to listen to

escuela *f* school

ese/esa that

esos/esas those

España *f* Spain

español(a) Spanish

especialidad *f* speciality

espectáculo *m* entertainment

espejo *m* mirror

esperar to wait (for) ; to hope

espuma *f* foam ; mousse *(for hair)*

esq. *abbrev. for* esquina

esquí *m* skiing ; ski

esquina *f* street corner

estación *f* station ; season
   estación de servicio petrol/service station

estacionar to park

estadio *m* stadium

Estados Unidos *mpl* United States

estanco *m* tobacconist's

estar to be

este *m* east

éste/esta this

estos/éstas these

estrecho(a) narrow

estrella *f* star

estropeado(a) out of order

estudiante *m/f* student

etiqueta *f* label ; ticket ; tag

euro *m* euro

Europa *f* Europe

evitar to avoid

examen *m* examination

explicar to explain

exportar to export

exposición *f* exhibition

exprimir to squeeze

extintor *m* fire extinguisher

extranjero(a) *m/f* foreigner

F

fábrica *f* factory

fácil easy

factura *f* receipt ; bill ; account

falda *f* skirt

familia *f* family

farmacia *f* chemist's ; pharmacy

faro *m* headlamp ; lighthouse

faros *mpl* headlights

favor *m* favour

febrero *m* February

fecha *f* date

feliz happy

feo(a) ugly

feria *f* trade fair ; funfair

ferrocarril *m* railway

festivos *mpl* public holidays

ficha *f* token ; counter *(in games)*

fichero *m* file *(computer)*

fiebre *f* fever

fiesta *f* party ; public holiday

fila *f* row ; line *(row, queue)*

fin *m* end

finca *f* farm ; country house

fino fine ; thin

firma *f* signature

firmar to sign

flor *f* flower

floristería *f* florist's shop

folleto *m* leaflet ; brochure

fonda *f* inn ; small restaurant

fontanero *m* plumber

formulario *m* form

foto *f* picture ; photo

fotocopiar to photocopy

frágil fragile

frambuesa *f* raspberry

freír to fry

frenar to brake

freno *m* brake

frente a opposite

fresa *f* strawberry

fresco(a) fresh ; crisp ; cool

frigorífico *m* fridge

frío(a) cold

frito(a) fried

fruta *f* fruit

frutos secos *mpl* nuts *(to eat)*

fuego *m* fire

fuera outdoors ; out

fuerte strong ; loud

fuga *f* leak *(of gas, liquid)*

fumadores *mpl* smokers

fumar to smoke

funcionar to work ; to function

funcionario(a) *m/f* civil servant

funda *f* case ; crown *(for tooth)* ; pillowcase

fusible *m* fuse

fútbol *m* football

G

gafas *fpl* glasses

galés(lesa) Welsh

Gales *m* Wales

gallego(a) Galician

galleta *f* biscuit

ganar to earn ; to win *(sports, etc)*

garaje *m* garage

garganta *f* throat

gaseosa *f* lemonade

gasoil *m* diesel fuel

gasóleo *m* diesel oil

gasolina *f* petrol
    gasolina sin plomo unleaded
    petrol

gasolinera *f* petrol station

gastar to spend *(money)*

gato *m* cat ; jack *(for car)*

gente *f* people

gerente *m/f* manager

girar to turn around

glorieta *f* roundabout

goma *f* rubber ; eraser

gordo(a) fat

gorra *f* cap *(hat)*

gorro *m* hat

gracias thank you

Gran Bretaña *f* Great Britain

grande large ; big ; tall

grandes almacenes *mpl*
    department store

granja *f* farm

granjero(a) *m/f* farmer

gratinar to grill

gratis free *(costing nothing)*

grave serious *(accident, etc)*

gripe *f* flu

gris grey

gritar to shout

grupo *m* group ; band *(rock)*

guantes *mpl* gloves

guapo(a) handsome ; attractive

guardar to put away ; to keep

guardarropa *m* cloakroom

guardería *f* nursery
    guardia infantil nursery school

guardia *f* guard

guerra *f* war

guía *m/f* courier ; guide

guiar to guide

gustar to like ; to enjoy

H

haba *f* broad bean

habitación *f* room

hablar (con) to speak/talk to

hacer to do ; to make

hacia toward(s)

harina *f* flour

hasta until ; till

hay there is/there are

hecho(a) finished ; done

helado *m* ice cream

herido(a) injured

herir to hurt

hermano(a) *m/f* brother/sister

hermoso(a) beautiful

herramienta *f* tool

hervido(a) boiled

hervir to boil

hielo *m* ice

hierba *f* grass ; herb

hierro *m* iron

hijo(a) *m/f* son/daughter

hilo *m* thread ; linen

hincha *m/f* fan *(football, etc)*

hinchado(a) swollen

hola hello ; hi!

hombre *m* man

hora *f* hour ; appointment
    hora punta rush hour

horario *m* timetable

horno *m* oven

hostal *m* small hotel ; hostel

hoy today

huelga *f* strike *(of workers)*

hueso *m* bone

huésped *m/f* guest

huevo *m* egg

humo *m* smoke

I

ida *f* outward journey
    de ida y vuelta return *(ticket)*

idioma *m* language

iglesia *f* church

igual equal

importante important

importe total *m* total *(amount)*

impreso *m* form

impuesto *m* tax

incendio *m* fire

incluido(a) included

incómodo(a) uncomfortable

indicaciones *fpl* directions

índice *m* index

infarto *m* heart attack

información *f* information

informe *m* report *(medical, police)*

ingeniero(a) *m/f* engineer

Inglaterra *f* England

inglés(lesa) English

ingredientes *mpl* ingredients

inquilino(a) *m/f* tenant

insolación *f* sunstroke

instituto *m* institute ; secondary
    school

instrucciones *fpl* instructions

instrumento *m* tool

Internet *m or f* internet

intérprete *m/f* interpreter

introducir to introduce ; to insert

invierno *m* winter

invitación *f* invitation

ir to go

Irlanda *f* Ireland

Irlanda del Norte *f* Northern Ireland

irlandés(desa) Irish

isla *f* island

itinerario *m* route ; schedule

izq./izqda. *abbrev. for* izquierda

izquierda *f* left

J

jabón *m* soap

jamás never

jamón *m* ham
    jamón serrano cured ham
    jamón (de) York boiled ham

jardín *m* garden

jarra *f* jug ; mug

jefe(a) *m/f* chief ; head ; boss

jerez *m* sherry

joven young

jubilado(a) *m/f* retired person

judías *fpl* beans

judío(a) Jew

juego *m* game

jueves *m* Thursday

juez(a) *m/f* judge

jugador(a) *m/f* player

jugar to play ; to gamble

julio *m* July

juguete *m* toy

junio *m* June

junto(a) together
  junto a next to

juventud *f* youth

K

kilo *m* kilo(gram)

kilómetro *m* kilometre

L

la the ; her ; it ; you *(formal)*

labio *m* lip

laborable working *(day)*

lado *m* side
  al lado de beside

ladrón(ona) *m/f* thief

lago *m* lake

lana *f* wool

lápiz *m* pencil

largo(a) long

lata *f* can *(container)* ; tin

lavabo *m* lavatory ; washbasin

lavado(a) washed
  lavado en seco dry-cleaning

lavadora *f* washing machine

lavandería *f* laundry ; launderette

lavavajillas *m* dishwasher

lavar(se) to wash (oneself)
  lavarse to wash oneself

leche *f* milk

lector de CD *m* CD player

leer to read

lejos far

lengua *f* language ; tongue

lente *f* lens
  lentes de contacto contact lenses

lentillas *fpl* contact lenses

lento(a) slow

letra *f* letter *(of alphabet)*

levantarse to get up ; to rise

ley *f* law

libra *f* pound *(currency, weight)*

libre free/vacant

librería *f* bookshop

libro *m* book

licencia *f* permit ; licence

ligero(a) light *(not heavy)*

limón *m* lemon

limpiar to clean

limpieza en seco *f* dry-cleaning

limpio(a) clean

liquidación *f* sales

liso(a) plain ; smooth

lista *f* list

listo(a) ready

litera *f* berth ; couchette ; sleeper

llamada *f* call

llamar to call ; to ring

llano(a) flat

llanta *f* tyre

llave *f* key ; tap ; spanner

llavero *m* keyring

Lleg. *abbrev. for* llegadas

llegada *f* arrival

llegar to arrive ; to come

llenar to fill ; to fill in

lleno(a) full (up)
  lleno, por favor fill it up, please

llevar to bring ; to wear ; to carry
  para llevar to take away

llorar to cry *(weep)*

lluvia *f* rain

local *m* premises ; bar

localidad *f* place

loncha *f* slice *(ham, etc)*

Londres *m* London

luces *fpl* lights

luchar to fight

lugar *m* place

lujo *m* luxury

luna *f* moon
  luna de miel honeymoon

lunes *m* Monday

luz *f* light

M

madera *f* wood

madrastra *f* stepmother

madre *f* mother

maduro(a) ripe ; mature

mal/malo(a) bad *(weather, news)*

maleta *f* case ; suitcase

malo(a) bad

mañana tomorrow

mañana *f* morning

mancha *f* stain ; mark

mandar to send
  mandar un mensaje de texto to text

manera *f* way ; manner

mano *f* hand
  de segunda mano secondhand

mantener to maintain ; to keep

mantequilla *f* butter

manzana *f* apple ; block *(of houses)*

mapa *m* map
  mapa de carreteras road map

máquina *f* machine

mar *m* sea

marca *f* brand ; make

marcar to dial

marcha *f* gear
  marcha atrás reverse gear

marco *m* picture frame

marea *f* tide

mareado(a) sick *(car, sea)* ; dizzy

marido *m* husband

marisquería *f* seafood restaurant

marrón brown

marroquí Moroccan

marroquinería *f* leather goods

martes *m* Tuesday

marzo *m* March

más more ; plus
  más que more than

matar to kill

matrícula *f* number plate

matrimonio *m* marriage

mayo *m* May

mayor bigger ; biggest
  mayor que bigger than
mecánico *m* mechanic
mechero *m* lighter
medianoche *f* midnight
medias *fpl* tights ; stockings
medicina *f* medicine ; drug
médico(a) *m/f* doctor
medida *f* measurement ; size
medio *m* the middle
medio(a) half
  media hora half an hour
mediodía *m* midday ; noon
medir to measure
Mediterráneo *m* Mediterranean
mejicano(a) *m/f* Mexican
Méjico *m* Mexico
mejor best ; better
  mejor que better than
melocotón *m* peach
melón *m* melon
menor smaller/smallest ; least
menos minus ; less ; except
  menos que less than
mensaje *m* message
  mensaje de texto text message
mensual monthly
menú *m* menu
  menú del día set menu
mercado *m* market
mercería *f* haberdasher's
merienda *f* afternoon snack
mermelada *f* jam
mes *m* month
mesa *f* table
mesón *m* traditional restaurant
metro *m* metre ; underground
mezclar to mix
mi my
miel *f* honey
mientras while
miércoles *m* Wednesday
migraña *f* migraine
mil thousand
minusválido(a) *m/f* disabled person
minuto *m* minute
mirar to look at ; to watch
mismo(a) same

mitad *f* half
mochila *f* backpack ; rucksack
moda *f* fashion
moderno(a) modern
modo *m* way ; manner
mojado(a) wet
molestar to disturb
moneda *f* currency ; coin
monedero *m* purse
montaña *f* mountain
montar to ride
morado(a) purple
mordedura *f* bite
morder to bite
morir to die
mosca *f* fly
mostrador *m* counter ; desk
mostrar to show
moto *f* (motor)bike ; moped
motocicleta *f* motorbike
motor *m* engine ; motor
móvil *m* mobile phone
mucho a lot ; much
mucho(a) a lot (of) ; much
muchos(as) many
muela *f* tooth
muelle *m* quay ; pier
muerto(a) dead
muestra *f* exhibition ; sample
mujer *f* woman ; wife
multa *f* fine *(to be paid)*
mundo *m* world
muro *m* wall
museo *m* museum ; art gallery
muy very

N

nacer to be born
nacimiento *m* birth
nacionalidad *f* nationality
nada nothing
  de nada don't mention it
nadar to swim
nadie nobody
naranja *f* orange
nariz *f* nose
nata *f* cream

natación *f* swimming
Navidad *f* Christmas
necesitar to need ; to require
negocios *mpl* business
negro(a) black
neumático *m* tyre
nevar to snow
nevera *f* refrigerator
nido *m* nest
niebla *f* fog
nieto(a) *m/f* grandson/daughter
nieve *f* snow
niña *f* girl ; baby girl
ningún/ninguno(a) none
niño *m* boy ; baby ; child
nivel *m* level ; standard
noche *f* night
Nochebuena *f* Christmas Eve
Nochevieja *f* New Year's Eve
nombre *m* name
  nombre de pila first name
norte *m* north
notario(a) *m/f* notary ; solicitor
noticias *fpl* news
novia *f* girlfriend ; fiancée ; bride
noviembre *m* November
novio *m* boyfriend ; fiancé ;
  bridegroom
nublado(a) cloudy
nudo *m* knot
nuestro(a) our ; ours
nuevo(a) new
número *m* number ; size ; issue
nunca never

O

o or
  o... o... either... or...
obligatorio(a) compulsory
obra *f* work ; play *(theatre)*
obstruido(a) blocked *(pipe)*
obtener to get *(to obtain)*
ocio *m* spare time
octubre *m* October
ocupado engaged
oeste *m* west
oferta *f* special offer

oficina *f* office

ofrecer to offer

oído *m* ear

oír to hear

ojo *m* eye

olor *m* smell

olvidar to forget

onda *f* wave

oportunidades *fpl* bargains

orden *f* command

orden *m* order

ordenador *m* computer

oreja *f* ear

organizar to arrange ; to organize

oro *m* gold

oscuro(a) dark ; dim

otoño *m* autumn ; fall

otro(a) other ; another
   otra vez again

P

padrastro *m* stepfather

padre *m* father

pagar to pay for ; to pay

página *f* page

país *m* country

paisaje *m* landscape ; countryside

pájaro *m* bird

palabra *f* word

palacio *m* palace

pan *m* bread ; loaf of bread

panadería *f* bakery

pañal *m* nappypantalones *mpl*
  trousers
   pantalones cortos shorts

pañuelo *m* handkerchief ; scarf

papel *m* paper
   papel higiénico toilet paper

papelería *f* stationer's

par even *(number)*

par *m* pair

para for ; towards

parada *f* stop

parado(a) unemployed

parador *m* state-run hotel

paraguas *m* umbrella

parar to stop

parecido(a) a similar to

pared *f* wall *(inside)*

pareja *f* couple *(2 people)*

parque *m* park

parrilla *f* grill ; barbecue
   a la parrilla grilled

particular private

partida *f* game ; departure
   partida de nacimiento birth
  certificate

partido *m* match *(sport)* ; party
  (political)

partir to depart

pasado(a) stale *(bread)* ; rotten

pasaje *m* ticket ; fare ; alleyway

pasajero(a) *m/f* passenger

pasar to happen

pasatiempo *m* hobby ; pastime

Pascua *f* Easter

paseo *m* walk ; avenue

pasta *f* pastry ; pasta
   pasta de dientes toothpaste

pastel *m* cake ; pie

pastelería *f* cake shop

pastilla *f* tablet ; pill

patata *f* potato
   patatas fritas french fries ; crisps

patinar to skate

paz *f* peace

p. ej. *abbrev. for* por ejemplo

peaje *m* toll

peatón/peatona *m/f* pedestrian

peces *mpl* fish

pedir to ask for ; to order
   pedir prestado to borrow

pegar to stick (on) ; to hit

peine *m* comb

película *f* film

peligroso(a) dangerous

pelo *m* hair

pelota *f* ball

peluquería *f* hairdresser's

pensar to think

pensión *f* guesthouse

peor worse ; worst

pequeño(a) little ; small ; tiny

pera *f* pear

perder to lose ; to miss *(train, etc)*

perdido(a) missing *(lost)*

perdonar to forgive

perezoso(a) lazy

perfecto(a) perfect

periódico *m* newspaper

permiso *m* permission ; pass ;
  permit ; licence

permitir to allow ; to let

pero but

perro *m* dog

persona *f* person

personal *m* staff

pesado(a) heavy ; boring

pesar to weigh

pescadería *f* fishmonger's

pescado *m* fish

pescar to fish

peso *m* weight ; scales

pez *m* fish

picado(a) chopped ; minced

picadura *f* insect bite ; sting

picar to itch ; to sting

pie *m* foot

piel *f* fur ; skin ; leather

pierna *f* leg

pieza *f* part ; room

pila *f* battery *(radio, etc)*

píldora *f* pill

pimienta *f* pepper *(spice)*

pinchar to have a puncture

pinchos *mpl* savoury titbits
   pinchos morunos kebabs

pintar to paint

pintura *f* paint ; painting

piscina *f* swimming pool

piso *m* floor ; storey ; flat

placa *f* licence plate

plancha *f* iron *(for clothes)*
   a la plancha grilled

planchar to iron

plano *m* plan ; town map

planta *f* plant ; floor ; sole *(of foot)*
   planta baja ground floor

plato *m* plate ; dish *(food)* ; course
   plato principal main course

playa *f* beach ; seaside

plaza *f* square *(in town)*

plazo *m* period ; expiry date

pobre poor

poco(a) little
poder to be able
podrido(a) rotten *(fruit, etc)*
policía *f* police
policía *m/f* policeman/woman
póliza *f* policy ; certificate
pollo *m* chicken
polvo *m* powder ; dust
pomada *f* ointment
poner to put
   poner en marcha to start *(car)*
por by ; per ; through ; about
   por adelantado in advance
   por correo by mail
porque because
postal *f* postcard
postre *m* dessert ; pudding
potable drinkable
precio *m* price ; cost
precioso(a) lovely
preferir to prefer
prefijo *m* dialling code
pregunta *f* question
preguntar to ask
premio *m* prize
preocupado(a) worried
preparar to prepare ; to cook
presentar to introduce
presión *f* pressure
prestar to lend
primavera *f* spring *(season)*
primer/o(a) first
primo(a) *m/f* cousin
principal main
principiante *m/f* beginner
privado(a) private
probador *m* changing room
probar to try ; to taste
probarse to try on *(clothes)*
procedente de... coming from...
productos *mpl* produce ; products
profesor(a) *m/f* teacher
profundo(a) deep
prohibido(a) prohibited/no...
prometer to promise
prometido(a) engaged
pronto soon

propietario(a) *m/f* owner
propina *f* tip
propio(a) own
provisional temporary
próximo(a) next
público(a) public
pueblo *m* village ; country
puente *m* bridge
puerta *f* door ; gate
puerto *m* port
puesto que since
pulsera *f* bracelet

Q

que than ; that ; which
¿qué? what? ; which?
   ¿qué tal? how are you?
quedar to remain ; to be left
   quedar bien to fit *(clothes)*
queja *f* complaint
quemar to burn
querer to want ; to love
   querer decir to mean
querido(a) dear *(on letter)*
queso *m* cheese
¿quién? who?
quitar to remove
quizá(s) perhaps

R

ración *f* portion
rama *f* branch *(of tree)*
ramo *m* bunch *(of flowers)*
rápido(a) quick ; fast
rato *m* a while
ratón *m* mouse
razón *f* reason
real royal
rebajas *fpl* sale(s)
recambio *m* spare ; refill
recargar to recharge *(battery, etc)*
receta *f* prescription ; recipe
recibir to receive
recibo *m* receipt
reclamación *f* claim ; complaint
recoger to collect
recogida *f* collection

recomendar to recommend
reconocer to recognize
recordar to remember
recuerdo *m* souvenir
red *f* net
redondo(a) round *(shape)*
reducción *f* reduction
reducir to reduce
reembolso *m* refund
refresco *m* refreshment ; drink
regalo *m* gift ; present
régimen *m* diet
regla *f* period *(menstruation)* ; ruler
reina *f* queen
Reino Unido *m* United Kingdom
reírse to laugh
rellenar to fill in
reloj *m* clock ; watch
reparación *f* repair
reparar to repair
repetir to repeat
repuestos *mpl* spare parts
reserva *f* booking(s) ; reservation
reservar to reserve ; to book
resfriado *m* cold *(illness)*
responder to answer ; to reply
respuesta *f* answer
restaurante *m* restaurant
resto *m* the rest
retraso *m* delay
retrato *m* portrait
reunión *f* meeting
revelar to develop *(photos)*
revisar to check
revisión *f* car service ; inspection
revista *f* magazine
rey *m* king
rico(a) rich *(person)*
rincón *m* corner
río *m* river
robar to steal
rodeado(a) de surrounded by
rodilla *f* knee
rojo(a) red
romper to break ; to tear
ropa *f* clothes
rosa *f* rose

rosa pink
roto(a) broken
rotonda *f* roundabout *(traffic)*
rubio(a) blond ; fair haired
rueda *f* wheel
ruido *m* noise

S

sábado *m* Saturday
sábana *f* sheet *(bed)*
saber to know *(facts)* ; to know how
sabor *m* taste ; flavour
sacar to take out *(of bag, etc)*
sagrado(a) holy
sal *f* salt
sala *f* hall ; hospital ward
salado(a) savoury ; salty
salario *m* wage
saldos *mpl* sales
salida *f* exit/departure
salir to go out ; to come out
saltar to jump
salteado(a) sauté ; sautéed
salud *f* health
    ¡salud! cheers!
salvar to save *(life)*
santo(a) saint ; holy ; saint's day
secar to dry
seco(a) dry ; dried *(fruit, beans)*
secretario(a) *m/f* secretary
seda *f* silk
seguida: en seguida straight away
seguir to continue ; to follow
según according to
segundo(a) second
    de segunda mano secondhand
seguramente probably
seguro *m* insurance
seguro(a) safe ; certain
sello *m* stamp *(postage)*
semáforo *m* traffic lights
semana *f* week
    Semana Santa Holy Week
señal *f* sign ; signal ; road sign
sencillo(a) simple ; single *(ticket)*
señor *m* gentleman
    Señor (Sr.) Mr ; Sir
señora *f* lady

Señora (Sra.) Mrs ; Ms ; Madam
señoras ladies
señorita *f* Miss
    Señorita (Srta.)... Miss...
sentarse to sit
sentir to feel
septiembre *m* September
ser to be
servicio *m* service ; service charge
    servicios toilets
sesión *f* performance ; screening
si if
sí yes
sida *m* AIDS
siempre always
siento: lo siento I'm sorry
siglo *m* century
siguiente following ; next
silla *f* chair ; seat
    silla de ruedas wheelchair
sillón *m* armchair
simpático(a) nice ; kind
sin without
    sin plomo unleaded
sitio *m* place ; space ; position
sobre on ; upon ; about
sobre *m* envelope
sobrino(a) *m/f* nephew/niece
socio(a) *m/f* member ; partner
¡socorro! help!
sol *m* sun ; sunshine
solo(a) alone ; lonely
sólo only
soltero(a) single *(unmarried)*
sombra *f* shade ; shadow
sombrero *m* hat
sonrisa *f* smile
sordo(a) deaf
sótano *m* basement
Sr. *abbrev. for* señor
Sra. *abbrev. for* señora
Srta. *abbrev. for* señorita
su his/her/its/their/your
sucio(a) dirty
sudar to sweat
suegro(a) *m/f* father/mother-in-law
suelo *m* soil ; ground ; floor

sueño *m* dream
suerte *f* luck
superior higher
sur *m* south
surtidor *m* petrol pump
sus his/her/their/your

T

tabla *f* board
    tabla de planchar ironing board
tacón *m* heel *(shoe)*
TALGO *m* Intercity express train
talla *f* size
taller *m* garage *(for repairs)*
talón *m* heel ; counterfoil ; stub
talonario *m* cheque book
también as well ; also ; too
tampoco neither
tapas *fpl* appetizers ; snacks
taquilla *f* ticket office
tarde *f* evening ; afternoon
tarde late
tarjeta *f* card
    tarjeta de crédito credit card
    tarjeta telefónica phonecard
tasca *f* bar ; cheap restaurant
taza *f* cup
té *m* tea
techo *m* ceiling
tejado *m* roof
tela *f* material ; fabric
telefonear to phone
teléfono *m* phone
    (teléfono) móvil mobile (phone)
televisor *m* television set
temporal *m* storm
temprano(a) early
tenedor *m* fork *(for eating)*
tener to have
    tener miedo de to be afraid of
    tener morriña to be homesick
    tener que to have to
    tener razón to be right
terremoto *m* earthquake
tía *f* aunt
tiempo *m* time ; weather
tienda *f* store ; shop ; tent
tierra *f* earth

tijeras *fpl* scissors

timbre *m* doorbell ; official stamp

tinta *f* ink

tinto *m* red wine

tintorería *f* dry-cleaner's

tío *m* uncle

tipo *m* sort
  tipo de cambio exchange rate

tique *m* ticket

tirar to throw (away) ; to pull

tire pull

tirita *f* (sticking) plaster

toalla *f* towel

tocar to touch ; to play (*instrument*)

todo(a) all
  todo everything
  todo el mundo everyone

tomar to take ; to have (*food/drink*)

tonto(a) stupid

tormenta *f* thunderstorm

toro *m* bull

torre *f* tower

torta *f* cake

tos *f* cough

toser to cough

trabajar to work (*person*)

trabajo *m* work

traducción *f* translation

traducir to translate

traer to fetch ; to bring

tragar to swallow

traje *m* suit ; outfit
  traje de baño swimsuit

tranquilo(a) calm ; quiet

tras after ; behind

tren *m* train

triste sad

trozo *m* piece

tumbarse to lie down

tumbona *f* deckchair

turista *m/f* tourist

U

Ud(s). *abbrev for* usted(es)

últimamente lately

último(a) last

ultramarinos *m* grocery shop

un(a) a/an

uña *f* nail (*finger, toe*)

únicamente only

Unión Europea *f* European Union

unos(as) some

urgencias *fpl* casualty department

usar to use

uso *m* use ; custom

útil useful

utilizar to use

uva *f* grape

V

vacaciones *fpl* holiday

vale OK

vale... it's worth...

vale *m* token ; voucher

válido(a) valid (*ticket, licence, etc*)

vapor *m* steam
  al vapor steamed

variado(a) assorted ; mixed

varios(as) several

vasco(a) Basque

vaso *m* glass (*for drinking*)

veces *fpl* times

vecino(a) *m/f* neighbour

velocidad *f* speed

vendedor(a) *m/f* salesman/woman

vender to sell

venenoso(a) poisonous

venir to come

venta *f* sale ; country inn

ventana *f* window

ventilador *m* fan (*electric*)

ver to see ; to watch

verano *m* summer

verdad *f* truth
  ¿de verdad? really?

verde green

verduras *fpl* vegetables

vestido *m* dress

vestirse to get dressed

vez *f* time

vía *f* track ; rails ; platform
  por vía oral/bucal orally

viajar to travel

viaje *m* journey ; trip

vida *f* life

vidrio *m* glass (*substance*)

viejo(a) old

viento *m* wind

viernes *m* Friday
  Viernes Santo Good Friday

viña *f* vineyard

vino *m* wine

visa *f* visa

visita *f* visit

víspera *f* eve

viudo(a) *m/f* widow/widower

vivir to live

volar to fly

volver to come/go back ; to return

voz *f* voice

vuelo *m* flight

vuelta *f* turn ; return ; change
  (*money*)

vuestro(a) your (*plural with friends*)

W

wáter *m* lavatory ; toilet

Y

y and

yate *m* yacht

yerno *m* son-in-law

yo I ; me

Z

zapatería *f* shoe shop

zapatillas *fpl* slippers
  zapatillas de deporte trainers

zapato *m* shoe

zona *f* zone
  zona azul controlled parking area

zumo *m* juice

Reference Zone

This section gives you the nuts and bolts –
everything from alphabet and numbers to
telling the time, plus the grammar bits
including nouns, adverbs, pronouns and verb
tables. Each topic has its own track and is
illustrated with examples.

Alphabet (a, b, c)

The Spanish alphabet is nearly the same as the English one, though it has another letter ñ. It comes after n in alphabetical order.

Traditionally, **ch**, **ll** and **rr** were considered separate letters, and so they too have names. As Spanish people sometimes still use these names, their pronunciation is included. The accents on Spanish vowels, unlike French ones, are always 'acute': **á, é, í, ó, ú**. They are used either to show stress, or to differentiate between words that are otherwise spelt the same, such as **tú** 'you' and **tu** 'your'.

a	*a*	n	***en***-*ay*
b	*bay*	ñ	***en***-*yay*
c	*thay*	o	*o*
ch	*tchay*	p	*pay*
d	*de*	q	*koo*
e	*ay*	r	***e***-*ray*
f	***e***-*fay*	rr	***e***-*rray*
g	*khay*	s	***ess***-*ay*
h	***atch***-*ay*	t	*tay*
i	*ee*	u	*oo*
j	***kho***-*ta*	v	***oo***-*bay*
k	*ka*	w	***oo***-*bay* ***dob***-*lay*
l	***el***-*ay*	x	***ek***-*eess*
ll	***el***-*yay*	y	*ee gree*-***ay***-*ga*
m	***em***-*ay*	z	***thet***-*a*

how do you spell 'house'?	**¿cómo se escribe 'casa'?**
	*ko-mo say ess-**kree**-bay **ka**-sa?*
it's spelt with a b	**se escribe con b**
	*say ess-**kree**-bay kon bay*
in capitals	**en mayúsculas**
	*en ma-**yoo**-skoo-lass*
in small letters	**en minúsculas**
	*en mee-**noo**-skoo-lass*
full stop/comma	**punto/coma**
	***poon**-to/**ko**-ma*

> **need to know**
>
> Spanish letters are feminine so it's una A 'an A', una B 'a B' and so on.

Numbers (1, 2, 3 ...)

In grammar terms, these are known as 'cardinals' and they operate the same way in Spanish as in English. Some differences occur in the way they are written.

In Spanish, prices and decimals are written with a comma instead of the dot we use in English, while thousands are separated by a full stop rather than a comma:

700,000 **700.000,**
a 1.6 litre engine **un motor de 1,6 litros**

'Hundred' is **cien** when counting or before a noun (**cien soldados** 'one hundred soldiers') or specifying a number of thousands or millions: **cien mil** 'one hundred thousand', **cien millones** 'one hundred million'. But when adding smaller numbers onto one hundred it's **ciento uno**, **ciento dos** and so on. The numbers **doscientos**, **trescientos**, etc become **doscientas**, **trescientas**, etc with feminine nouns.

---

need to know

Currency symbols such as the euro and dollar signs (€, $) tend to be given after the number, rather than before as in English.

0	cero **ther**-o
1	uno **oo**-no
2	dos *doss*
3	tres *tress*
4	cuatro **kwa**-tro
5	cinco **theenk**-o
6	seis **say**-eess
7	siete **syet**-ay
8	ocho **otch**-o
9	nueve **nweb**-ay
10	diez *dyeth*
11	once **onth**-ay
12	doce **doth**-ay
13	trece **treth**-ay
14	catorce ka-**torth**-ay
15	quince **keenth**-ay
16	dieciséis dyeth-ee-**say**-eess
17	diecisiete dyeth-ee-**syet**-ay
18	dieciocho dyeth-ee-**otch**-o

19	diecinueve *dyeth-ee-**nweb**-ay*
20	veinte ***bayn**-tay*
21	veintiuno *bayn-tee-**oo**-no*
22	veintidós / veinte y dos *bayn-tee-**doss***
23	veintitrés / veinte y tres *bayn-tee-**tress***
24	veinticuatro / veinte y cuatro *bayn-tee-**kwat**-ro*
25	venticinco / veinte y cinco *bayn-tee-**theenk**-o*
26	veintiséis / veinte y seis *bayn-tee-**say**-eess*
30	treinta ***tray**-een-ta*
31	treinta y uno *tray-een-ta-ee-**oon**-o*
40	cuarenta *kwa-**ren**-ta*
50	cincuenta *theen-**kwen**-ta*
60	sesenta *se-**sen**-ta*
70	setenta *se-**ten**-ta*
80	ochenta *otch-**en**-ta*
90	noventa *no-**ben**-ta*
100	cien *thyen*
101	ciento uno ***thyen**-to **oo**-no*
110	ciento diez ***thyen**-to **dyeth***
200	doscientos *doss-**thyen**-toss*
250	doscientos cincuenta *doss-**thyen**-toss theenk-**wen**-ta*
300	trescientos *tress-**thyen**-toss*
400	cuatrocientos ***kwat**-ro-**thyen**-toss*
500	quinientos *keen-**yen**-toss*
600	seiscientos *say-eess-**thyen**-toss*
700	sietecientos *syet-ay-**thyen**-toss*
800	ochocientos *otch-o-**thyen**-toss*
900	novecientos *no-bay-**thyen**-toss*
1,000	mil *meel*
2,000	dos mil *doss meel*
1,000,000	un millón *oon meel-**yon***

there are nine of us	somos nueve
	***som**-oss **nweb**-ay*
on page nineteen	en la página diecinueve
	*en la **pa**-khee-na dyeth-ee-**nweb**-ay*
I'm twenty years old	tengo veinte años
	***ten**-go **bayn**-tay **an**-yoss*

need to know

With people's ages, you have to use the word años - you can't leave it out as you do in English 'she's thirty', tiene treinta años.

Numbers (1st, 2nd, 3rd)

In grammar terms, these are known as 'ordinals' since they show the order that things come in. When used with a noun, they come before the noun and must agree with it.

first	**primer(o)**		sixth	**sexto**
	*pree-**mer**-o*			***sek**-sto*
second	**segundo**		seventh	**séptimo**
	*se-**goon**-do*			***sep**-tee-mo*
third	**tercer(o)**		eighth	octavo
	*ter-**ther**-o*			*ok-**ta**-bo*
fourth	**cuarto**		ninth	**noveno**
	***kwar**-to*			*no-**ben**-o*
fifth	**quinto**		tenth	**décimo**
	***keen**-to*			***deth**-ee-mo*

Primero (first) and **tercero** (third) are shortened to **primer** and **tercer** before a masculine singular noun:

the first chapter **el primer capítulo**
the third man **el tercer hombre**

> **need to know**
>
> In dates both primero and uno can be used for the first of the month.
> After that it is the numbers, dos, tres, and so on.

on the first of December **el uno de diciembre**
*el **oo**-no day deeth-**yem**-bray*

on the third of May **el tres de mayo**
*el tress day **ma**-yo*

5th November 2006 **5 de noviembre de 2006**
***theen**-ko day nob-**yem**-bray day doss meel **say**-eess*

Time (telling the time)

When talking about clock time and the time of day, 'time' is translated by **la hora**, which also means 'hour'.

Although in English we always say 'it's' and the time, in Spanish you only use **es** for times involving **la una** 'one o'clock'. For all other times, you use **son** (literally 'they are'):

it's one o'clock **es la una**
it's two o'clock **son las dos**

For times 'to' the hour, you use **menos**:

it's ten to eight **son las ocho menos diez**
at quarter to seven **a las siete menos cuarto**

For times 'past' the hour, you use **y**:

it's a quarter past one **es la una y cuarto**
it's ten past three **son las tres y diez**

The 24-hour clock is used particularly for train, bus and plane timetables and cinema times. The minutes past the hour are given from 1 to 59, and **quince** and **treinta** are used instead of **cuarto** and **media**:

it's six pm **son las dieciocho**
twenty fifteen (20:15) **las veinte quince**

---

need to know

When using the 12-hour clock, you can use **de la mañana (in the morning)**, **de la tarde (in the afternoon)** and **de la noche (at night)** to distinguish between am and pm.

---

what time is it?	**¿qué hora es?**
	*kay **o**-ra ess?*
it's 11pm	**son las once de la noche**
	*son lass **on**-thay day la **notch**-ay*
at what time?	**¿a qué hora?**
	*a kay **o**-ra?*
at midnight	**a medianoche**
	*a med-ee-a-**notch**-ay*
at midday, at noon	**a mediodía**
	*a med-ee-o-**dee**-a*

Time (in general)

 appears at top right containing **5**

The word 'time' covers a lot of meanings in English: 'time is money', 'three times', 'what time is it?' These senses of the word all have different translations in Spanish.

'Time' in general is **el tiempo**:
> **no tengo tiempo** I haven't got time

'Time' in the sense of 'occasion' is **la vez**:
> **la primera vez** the first time
> **la última vez** the last time

Both **en** and **dentro de** can be used to specify a length of time, but the meaning is different:
> **lo haré dentro de tres semanas** I'll do it in three weeks (three weeks from now)
> **lo hice en tres semanas** I did it in three weeks (in the space of three weeks)

Hace is used to mean 'ago':
> **lo compré hace una semana/un año** I bought it a week/a year ago

To translate 'since' in expressions of time, use **desde**:
> **estudio español desde septiembre** I've been studying Spanish since September

Desde can also mean 'from':
> **desde las ocho hasta las diez** from 8 to 10 o'clock

when?	**¿cuándo?** *kwan-do?*
sometimes	**algunas veces** or **a veces** *al-goo-nass beth-ess* or *a beth-ess*
often	**muchas veces** or **con frecuencia** *mootch-ass beth-ess* or *kon frek-wenth-ya*
all the time	**todo el tiempo** *tod-o el tyem-po*
from time to time	**de vez en cuando** *day beth en kwan-do*
on time	**a tiempo** *a tyem-po*
it's early	**es temprano** *ess tem-pra-no*
it's late	**es tarde** *ess tar-day*

Days of the week

Days of the week are masculine and the Spanish for 'day' is **el día**.

Monday	**lunes**		Friday	**viernes**
	loo-ness			**byer**-ness
Tuesday	**martes**		Saturday	**sábado**
	mar-tess			*sa*-ba-do
Wednesday	**miércoles**		Sunday	**domingo**
	myer-kol-ess			do-**meen**-go
Thursday	**jueves**			
	khwe-bess			

To say that something happens *on* Monday, you use **el** before the day of the week:

voy a Madrid el lunes I'm going to Madrid on Monday

If you want to say that something happens on Mondays/every Monday, you use **los**:

voy a Madrid los lunes I go to Madrid on Mondays (every Monday)

The article is also used when giving a range of days:

del lunes 17 al viernes 28 de enero from Monday 17 to Friday 28 January

every day	**todos los días**
	tod-oss loss **dee**-ass
last Tuesday	**el martes pasado**
	el **mar**-tess pa-**sa**-do
next Friday	**el viernes que viene** *or* **el próximo viernes**
	el **byer**-ness kay **byen**-ay or el **prok**-see-mo **byer**-ness
this Saturday	**este sábado**
	ess-tay **sa**-ba-do
today	**hoy**
	oy
tomorrow	**mañana**
	man-**ya**-na
yesterday	**ayer**
	a-**yer**
what day is it?	**¿qué día es?**
	kay **dee**-a ess

Months and seasons

Months are masculine in Spanish and the Spanish for 'month' is **el mes**.

January	**enero** *en-**er**-o*	July	**julio** ***khool**-yo*
February	**febrero** *feb-**rer**-o*	August	**agosto** *ag-**ost**-o*
March	**marzo** ***marth**-o*	September	**septiembre** *sept-**yem**-bray*
April	**abril** *ab-**reel***	October	**octubre** *ok-**too**-bray*
May	**mayo** ***ma**-yo*	November	**noviembre** *nob-**yem**-bray*
June	**junio** ***khoon**-yo*	December	**diciembre** *deeth-**yem**-bray*
spring	**la primavera** *la pree-ma-**ber**-a*	autumn	**el otoño** *el o-**ton**-yo*
summer	**el verano** *el be-**ra**-no*	winter	**el invierno** *el eenb-**yer**-no*

> **need to know**
>
> **Months and seasons are not written with a capital letter in Spanish.**

what's the date?	**¿qué es hoy?** *kay ess oy?*
in February	**en febrero** *en feb-**re**-ro*
in 2006	**en 2006 (dos mil seis)** *en doss meel **say**-eess*
Monday 26 February	**lunes veintiséis de febrero** ***loo**-ness bay-een-tee-**say**-eess day feb-**rer**-o*
my birthday is on 7 May	**mi cumpleaños es el siete de mayo** *mee koom-play-**an**-yoss ess el **syet**-ay day **ma**-yo*
in spring/in winter	**en primavera/en invierno** *en pree-ma-**ber**-a/en eenb-**yer**-no*

Colours

Colours can be used as adjectives or nouns. When used as adjectives, they usually agree with the noun they describe. Unlike in English, Spanish colours always follow the noun.

black	**negro(a)** *neg-ro(a)*	grey	**gris** *greess*
blue	**azul** *ath-ool*	orange	**naranja** *na-ran-kha*
brown	**marrón** *ma-rron*	pink	**rosa** *ro-sa*
red	**rojo(a)** *rokh-o(a)*	yellow	**amarillo(a)** *a-ma-ree-yo(a)*
green	**verde** *ber-day*	white	**blanco(a)** *blan-ko(a)*

need to know

Some colours, such as naranja **and** rosa**, are 'invariable', which means that they never change their endings. This also applies to colours made up of more than one word, for example 'a navy blue skirt'** una falda azul marino.

what colour is it?	**¿de qué color es?** *day kay ko-lor ess?*
a yellow jersey	**un jersey amarillo** *oon kher-say a-ma-ree-yo*
some black cars	**unos coches negros** *oo-noss kotch-ess neg-ross*
light/dark	**claro/oscuro** *kla-ro/oss-koo-ro*
a light green dress	**un vestido verde claro** *oon bess-tee-do ber-day kla-ro*

Quantities (a litre, a kilo, a tin)

9

Quantities are followed by **de**:

a litre of wine	**un litro de vino** *oon **lee**-tro day **bee**-no*
half a litre of milk	**medio litro de leche** *med-yo **lee**-tro day **letch**-ay*
100 grammes of sugar	**cien gramos de azúcar** *thyen **gra**-moss day a-**thoo**-kar*
half a kilo of sausage	**medio kilo de chorizo** *med-yo **kee**-lo day tcho-**reeth**-o*
a kilo of potatoes	**un kilo de patatas** *oon **kee**-lo day pa-**ta**-tass*
a quarter (kilo) of cheese	**un cuarto de queso** *oon **kwar**-to day **kay**-so*
a bottle of water	**una botella de agua** ***oo**-na bo-**te**-ya day **ag**-wa*
a tin of tomatoes	**una lata de tomates** ***oo**-na **la**-ta day to-**ma**-tess*
a packet of biscuits	**un paquete de galletas** *oon pu-**ket**-ay day ga-**ye**-tass*
a carton of orange juice	**un cartón de zumo de naranja** *oon kar-**ton** day **thoo**-mo day na-**ran**-kha*
a jar of jam	**un tarro de mermelada** *oon **ta**-rro day mer-me-**la**-da*
two slices of cured ham	**dos lonchas de jamón serrano** *doss **lontch**-ass day kha-**mon** se-**rra**-no*
a loaf of bread	**una barra de pan** ***oo**-na **ba**-rra day pan*
more ...	**más ...** *mass ...*
less ...	**menos ...** ***men**-oss ...*
enough ...	**bastante** *or* **suficiente ...** *ba-**stan**-tay or soo-feeth-**yen**-tay ...*

Nouns and articles (a cat)

Nouns are words that name things. 'Car', 'town', 'boy', 'day' and 'hope' are all common nouns; 'Madrid' and 'Jane' are proper nouns and written with a capital letter. In Spanish all nouns have 'gender', meaning they are either masculine or feminine.

The word you use for 'the' (el, la, los, las), and 'a', 'an' or 'some' (un, una, unos, unas) depends on whether the noun is masculine or feminine and singular or plural. El and un are used before masculine singular nouns; la and una are used before feminine singular nouns; los and unos are used before masculine plural nouns; and las and unas are used before feminine plural nouns. In grammar, the words for 'the' and 'a' are called 'articles'.

masculine singular
the book el libro
a book un libro

masculine plural
the books los libros
some books unos libros

feminine singular
the table la mesa
a table una mesa

feminine plural
the tables las mesas
some tables unas mesas

Most words for male people or animals are masculine in gender while most words for females are feminine, though not always; for example, la persona (the person) can refer to either a male or a female. When it comes to things, you just have to learn the gender, but sometimes you can make an educated guess from the noun ending.

Most nouns ending in -o are masculine, as are most words ending in consonants (apart from -d and -z):

el libro book
el río river
el lunes Monday
el tenedor fork
el reloj watch

Most nouns ending in -a are feminine, as are those with the following endings: -ción, -sión, -dad, -tad, -tud and -z:

la casa house
la televisión television
la verdad truth
la certitud certainty
la vez time (occasion)

10

Here are some common exceptions:

    el día day
    el mapa map
    la mano hand
    la radio radio

> **need to know**
>
> **Note that with feminine nouns beginning with a stressed a- or ha-, such as agua 'water' or hambre 'hunger', you use el, not la, so el agua and el hambre. However, in the plural, the article is las, so las aguas, not los.**

When there is more than one of something, the plural form is used. In English, this most often involves adding an -s to the singular noun (dogs, houses, markets), though some words have irregular plurals (man – men; mouse – mice; child – children). Adding an -s is also the way to make most Spanish words plural:

    el novio – los novios boyfriend – boyfriends
    la novia – las novias girlfriend – girlfriends

Where a Spanish noun ends in a consonant as opposed to a vowel, then the plural ending is **-es**:

    el color – los colores colour – colours
    el tren – los trenes train – trains
    la ciudad – las ciudades city – cities

Some words ending in **-s** are the same in the plural:

    el lunes – los lunes Monday – Mondays
    la crisis – las crisis crisis – crises

To form the plural of a word ending in **-z**, change the **-z** into **-ces**:

    el lápiz – los lápices pencil – pencils
    la vez – las veces time – times

> **need to know**
>
> **In the case of a mixed sex group, males take precedence, and you use the masculine form.**

Adjectives (small, happy)

Adjectives are 'describing' words that tell you more about a person or thing, such as size or colouring. Spanish adjectives agree with the noun they describe.

Most Spanish adjectives go after the noun they describe, but some very common adjectives usually come before the noun: **bueno**, **malo**, **alguno**, **ninguno**, **uno**, **primero** and **tercero**. These adjectives lose their final -o before a masculine singular noun.

Spanish adjectives agree with the nouns they describe and it is important to know how to make adjectives agree. Bear in mind that dictionaries often just give the masculine singular form.

	masculine singular/plural	feminine singular/plural
little	**pequeño/pequeños**	**pequeña/pequeñas**
old	**viejo/viejos**	**vieja/viejas**

If an adjective ends in any vowel other than -o, it doesn't change in the feminine:

clever	**inteligente/inteligentes**	**inteligente/inteligentes**
green	**verde/verdes**	**verde/verdes**

Many adjectives ending in a consonant in the masculine singular stay the same in the feminine singular. But to form the masculine and feminine plural of these, you add -es:

popular	**popular/populares**	**popular/populares**
present, current	**actual/actuales**	**actual/actuales**

Here are some adjective opposites:

big	**grande** *gran-day*	small	**pequeño** *pek-en-yo*
new	**nuevo** *nweb-o*	old	**viejo** *byekh-o*
first	**primero** *pree-mer-o*	last	**último** *ool-tee-mo*
good	**bueno** *bwen-o*	bad	**malo** *mal-o*
fast	**rápido** *rap-ee-do*	slow	**lento** *len-to*

> **need to know**
>
> **Adjectives ending in -z in the singular change to -ces in the plural,**
> **feliz – felices 'happy'.**

Possessives (my, mine, our)

Possessive adjectives are words like 'my', 'her' and 'our': 'my car', 'my husband'. Possessive pronouns are words such as 'mine', 'ours' and 'theirs', and stand in for a particular person or thing.

	masculine singular	feminine singular	masculine plural	feminine plural
my	mi	mi	mis	mis
your (for **tú**)	tu	tu	tus	tus
his, her, its, your (for **usted**)	su	su	sus	sus
our	nuestro	nuestra	nuestros	nuestras
your (for **vosotros/as**)	vuestro	vuestra	vuestros	vuestras
their, your (for **ustedes**)	su	su	sus	sus

Possessive adjectives, like other adjectives, must agree with the person or thing they describe: my letter **mi carta**; my letters **mis cartas**; our children **nuestros hijos**; our house **nuestra casa**.

Spanish has a second set of possessive adjectives that can be used after **ser** or after a noun. They also have to agree with the person or thing they describe:

(of) mine **mío(a)**
(of) yours **tuyo(a)**
(of) his, hers, its, yours **suyo(a)**
(of) ours **nuestro(a)**
(of) yours **vuestro(a)**
(of) theirs, yours **suyo(a)**

Used in combination with **el**, **la**, and so on, these words become pronouns that can stand in for nouns. The article and the ending must agree with the noun they stand in for:

I prefer your car to mine **prefiero tu coche al mío**

their house is near ours	su casa está cerca de la nuestra
	*soo **kass**-a ess-**ta ther**-ka day la **nwess**-tra*
whose car is it? – it's mine	¿de quién es el coche? – es mío
	*day kyen ess el **kotch**-ay? – ess **mee**-o*
a friend of ours	un amigo nuestro
	*oon a-**mee**-go **nwess**-tro*
his wife and mine	su mujer y la mía
	*soo moo-**kher** ee la **mee**-a*

Demonstratives (this, that)

Words like 'this', 'that', 'these' and 'those' are known as demonstratives. They can be used as adjectives before nouns, 'I like that car', or on their own as pronouns, 'I like that'.

The Spanish demonstrative adjectives are **este** 'this', **ese** 'that', and **aquel** 'that' (further away, 'yonder'), which have the following forms:

	masculine	feminine
this/these	este/estos	esta/estas
that/those *(close by)*	ese/esos	esa/esas
that/those *(further away)*	**aquel/aquellos**	**aquella/aquellas**

When used as pronouns, masculine and feminine demonstratives can be given an accent in Spanish: **éste/ésta/éstos/éstas**; **ése/ésa/ésos/ésas**; **aquél/aquélla/aquéllos/aquéllas**.

> **need to know**
>
> **When you are not referring to a specific object, 'that one', but rather to just 'that' in the abstract, you use a set of pronouns that are neither masculine nor feminine: esto, eso and aquello.**
> **¿qué es esto?** 'what's this?'

this year	**este año**
	*ess-tay **an**-yo*
that magazine	**esa revista**
	*ess-a reb-**ee**-sta*
those mountains	**aquellas montañas**
	*a-**ke**-yass mon-**tan**-yass*
this car is bigger than that one	**este coche es más grande que ése**
	*ess-tay **kotch**-ay ess mass **gran**-day kay **ess**-ay*
these pens and those ones over there	**estos bolígrafos y aquéllos**
	*ess-toss bo-**leeg**-ra-foss ee a-**ke**-yoss*
what's that?	**¿qué es eso?**
	*kay ess **ess**-o?*
what's that over there?	**qué es aquello?**
	*kay ess a-**ke**-yo?*

Prepositions (in, on, at)

Prepositions usually link something to a place, time or manner: '*in* the village', '*through* the tunnel', '*at* 8 o'clock', '*from* 9 *to* 5', '*in* a strange way'.

Prepositions don't always correspond exactly in Spanish and English. For example, while we 'depend *on* something', Spanish speakers **dependen** *de* **algo**. And although we often think of **en** as corresponding to 'in', it also corresponds to 'at' when someone is *at* a place: 'he's *at* home' **está en casa**.

need to know

Sometimes one language uses a preposition where it is not needed in the other. In English we 'look at photos' and 'listen to the radio' while Spanish speakers miran fotos **and** escuchan la radio.

Some common prepositions:

a	to, at
de	of, from
en	in, on, at
con	with
sin	without
entre	between
para	for (in terms of time, destination or purpose)
por	for, along, through, per, by, because of
desde	from, since

Remember that when **el** follows the prepositions **a** and **de**, they combine as follows:

a + el = al
al cine to the cinema
de + el = del
del presidente of the president, the president's

to go to Madrid by car	**ir a Madrid en coche** *eer a mad-**reed** en **kotch**-ay*
10 km from here	**a diez kilómetros de aquí** *a dyeth kee-**lo**-met-ross day a-**kee***
it's on the table	**está en la mesa** *ess-**ta** en la **mess**-a*

a room for two nights	**una habitación para dos noches** *oo-na a-bee-tath-**yon pa**-ra doss **notch**-ess*
a ticket to Madrid	**un billete para Madrid** *oon bee-**yet**-ay **pa**-ra mad-**reed***
a table for two	**una mesa para dos** *oo-na **mess**-a **pa**-ra doss*
thanks for the beer	**gracias por la cerveza** ***grath**-yass por la ther-**beth**-a*
through the park	**por el parque** *por el **par**-kay*
the price per night	**el precio por noche** *el **preth**-yo por **notch**-ay*
on the radio	**por la radio** *por la **rad**-yo*

---

need to know

Don't forget to put the so-called 'personal a' before words referring to people and pets, when they're the direct object (of any verb other than tener). 'I love Pablo' quiero a Pablo; 'I don't know his mother' no conozco a su madre; 'I didn't see anybody' no vi a nadie. There's no equivalent in English.

Questions (when? where? how?)

To ask a question in Spanish, simply take a statement and speak it in a questioning intonation, so **lo has hecho** 'you've done it' becomes **¿lo has hecho?** 'have you done it?' You can also ask a negative question using **no**: **¿no lo has hecho?** 'haven't you done it?'

For questions where the answer is not just a simple yes or no, use one of the various question words such as **¿cuándo?** when? and **¿dónde?** where?, not forgetting to add the accent that shows it's being used in a question.

---

need to know

In Spanish you need an opening upside-down question mark at the start of the question or the question part of the sentence.

how?	**¿cómo?** *ko-mo?*	how much?	**¿cuánto?** *kwan-to?*
who?	**¿quién?** *kyen?*	why?	**¿por qué?** *por kay?*

'Which' and 'what' can be either **qué** or **cual** (plural **cuáles**). Before a noun, use **qué**; otherwise use **cuál** (singular) or **cuáles** (plural). **Cuál** commonly implies a choice between a set of options, while **qué** asks for a definition or description of some kind.

which dress are you going to wear today?	**¿qué vestido te vas a poner hoy?** *kay bess-**tee**-do bass a po-**ner** oy?*
which is your house?	**¿cuál es tu casa?** *kwal ess too **kass**-a?*
which are your books?	**¿cuáles son tus libros?** ***kwal**-ess son tooss **leeb**-ross?*
what's your phone number?	**¿cuál es tu número de teléfono?** *kwal ess too **noo**-mer-o day te-**le**-fo-no?*
what's a search engine?	**¿qué es un buscador?** *kay ess oon boos-ka-**dor**?*
what did you do?	**¿qué hiciste?** *kay eeth-**eest**-ay?*
what did he say?	**¿qué dijo?** *kay **dee**-kho?*

Don't confuse **¿por qué?** *por kay?* 'why?' with **porque** *por-kay* 'because'. Remember that all Spanish question words take accents.

Negatives (no, not, never)

A negative question or statement is one containing 'not', 'never', 'no one', 'nobody', 'nothing', and so on.

In Spanish, any sentence can be made negative by placing the word **no** ('no' or 'not') before the verb:

I don't smoke **no fumo**

Juan doesn't study here **Juan no estudia aquí**

As in English, Spanish has several negative words, used with **no** or on their own before the verb:

never, not ... ever	**(no...) nunca** *(no...)* **noon**-*ka*
nobody, not ... anybody	**(no...) nadie** *(no...)* **nad**-*yay*
nothing, not ... anything	**(no...) nada** *(no...)* **na**-*da*
no longer, not ... anymore	**(no...) más** *(no...) mass*
not ... either	**(no...) tampoco** *(no...) tam-***pok**-*o*
no, not ... any	**(no...) ningún** *(no...) neen-***goon**
	(no...) ninguna *(no...) neen-***goon**-*a*
neither ... nor	**(no...) ni ... ni** *(no...) nee ... nee*

she never eats	**no come nunca** *or* **nunca come** *no* **ko**-*may* **noon**-*ka or* **noon**-*ka* **ko**-*may*
nobody spoke	**no habló nadie** *or* **nadie habló** *no ab-***lo** **nad**-*yay or* **nad**-*yay ab-***lo**
he no longer plays football	**no juega más al fútbol** *no* **khweg**-*a mass al* **foot**-*bol*
Pedro doesn't sing either	**Pedro no canta tampoco** **ped**-*ro no* **kan**-*ta tam-***po**-*ko*
neither Juan nor I smoke	**no fumamos ni Juan ni yo** *or* **ni Juan ni yo fumamos** *no foo-***ma**-*mos nee khwan nee yo or* *nee khwan nee yo foo-***ma**-*moss*

need to know

Some of these negative words can be used on their own as well:
'who was it? – nobody' ¿quién fue? – nadie; 'what have you done? – nothing' ¿qué has hecho? – nada.

Adverbs (slowly, kindly)

An adverb can describe a verb, adjective or other adverb: 'she walked *slowly*'; 'they are *extremely* ill'; 'they did *very well*'. It can also refer to a whole sentence and often tells you what the speaker is thinking or feeling: '*maybe* he's on holiday' and '*luckily*, we got there in time'.

In English, many adverbs are formed by adding -ly to an adjective, eg, 'sweetly' or 'quickly'. The Spanish equivalent of -ly is **-mente**, added to the feminine singular form of the adjective:

slow	**lento**	slowly	**lentamente**
kind	**amable**	kindly	**amablemente**

In Spanish, an adverbial phrase is often preferred to a single adverb. For example, using **con** with a noun, or **de modo** with an adjective:

carefully **cuidadosamente** *or* **con cuidado**
specatacularly **espectacularmente** *or* **de modo espectacular**

---

need to know

When two or more adverbs are used together and joined by y 'and' or **pero** 'but', the -mente is left off all but the last: 'he spoke slowly but clearly' habló lenta pero claramente.

Some adverbs do not follow any of the above rules. Here are some examples:

well	**bien** *byen*	worse	**peor** *pay-or*
badly	**mal** *mal*	often	**a menudo** *a men-oo-do*
much	**mucho** ***mootch**-o*	soon	**pronto** ***pron**-to*
little	**poco** ***po**-ko*	now	**ahora** *a-**or**-a*
more	**más** *mass*	also, as well, too	**también** *tamb-**yen***
less	**menos** ***men**-oss*	always	**siempre** ***syem**-pray*
better	**mejor** *mekh-**or***		

Pronouns (I, me, he)

Pronouns are words that stand in for nouns to avoid repetition, for example 'he' or 'him' instead of repeating someone's name.

Subject pronouns, tell you who is doing the action. Spanish often omits these entirely, since the verb endings usually show who the subject is. **Usted(es)** (formal 'you') is less often dropped since there is scope for confusion with 'he/she' and 'they'.

yo	I	**nosotros(as)**	we
tú	you (informal singular)	**vosotros(as)**	you (informal plural)
él	he	**ellos**	they (masculine or mixed)
ella	she	**ellas**	they (exclusively feminine)
usted	you (formal singular)	**ustedes**	you (formal plural)

In Spanish, there are no less than four words for 'you' (**tú**, **usted**, **vosotros(as)**, **ustedes**). When addressing one person, you use **tú** or **usted**. **Tú** is the form for friends, family and young people. It should not be used to an elderly stranger or someone in authority, in which case **usted** is more appropriate. For more than one person, **vosotros(as)** is the familiar form, and **ustedes** the formal. The verb form used with **usted** is the same as for 'he' and 'she' (and 'they' for **ustedes**). **Usted** and **ustedes** are sometimes shortened in writing to **Vd./Vds.** or **Ud./Uds.**

> **need to know**
>
> **With a mixed group of people, you use masculine pronouns rather than feminine ones, even when males are completely outnumbered.**

The set of pronouns used for the object of the sentence ('me', 'him', 'it', etc) are called object pronouns. There are also indirect object pronouns, used when a sentence has two objects, for example 'him' and 'it' in 'I bought him it'. One pronoun is more central to this sentence than the other. Since you can say 'I bought it' with the same meaning, whereas 'I bought him' means something different, then 'it' is the 'direct' object, and 'him' indirect. You can usually tell indirect pronouns by putting 'for' or 'to' in front of them: 'I bought him it' – 'I bought it for him'. Different words are needed in Spanish for these two sorts of pronoun.

Another set of pronouns is used after prepositions, much the same as the subject pronouns plus **mí** (me), **ti** (you) and **sí** (himself, herself, yourself, themselves or yourselves). Note that when these are combined with **con** 'with', they become **conmigo**, **contigo** or **consigo**: 'come with me' **ven conmigo**; 'they brought it with them' **lo trajeron consigo**.

	direct object	indirect object	after prepositions
me	me	me	mí
you (informal singular)	te	te	ti
him/it/you (masc)	lo	le	él
her/it/you (fem)	la	le	ella
			sí herself/itself/oneself/yourself
			usted you (formal singular)
us	nos	nos	nosotros(as)
you (informal plural)	os	os	vosotros(as)
them/yourselves (masc)	los	les	ellos
them/yourselves (fem)	las	les	ellas
			sí themselves/yourselves
			ustedes you (formal plural)

Object pronouns normally come before the verb, but with an infinitive, a gerund (the -ando or -iendo form), or an imperative (commands), they are usually tacked onto the end of verb to form one word.

In negative commands (telling someone not to do something), the pronoun comes before the verb.

With two object pronouns the indirect one comes before the direct one. Note that le and les become se when followed immediately by lo, los, la or las: 'I gave it to him' se lo di; 'I will send them to him' se los enviaré. Because se can mean so many things, a phrase like a él 'to him', a ella 'to her', or a usted 'to you' can be added for clarity.

is that you? – yes, it's me	¿eres tú? – sí, soy yo
	er-ess too? – see, soy yo
help me!	¡ayúdame!
	a-yoo-da-may!
don't touch it	no lo toques
	no lo tok-ess
I want to see it	quiero verlo or lo quiero ver
	kyer-oo ber-lo or lo kyer-o ber
he gave it to me	me lo dio
	me lo dyo
I'll give it to her, not to you	se lo daré a ella, no a usted
	say lo da-ray a ey-a, no a oo-sted

Verbs (to be, to see, to do)

Verbs are the 'doing words' that describe the action in a sentence. In Spanish, verb endings vary according to who is doing the action (the 'subject') and when the action happens (the 'tense'). In English we see something similar when we compare 'I go' and 'he goes', 'they go' and 'they went'.

The form in which you look up a verb in the dictionary is known as the infinitive. This is the base form of the verb, a form that is not restricted to any person or tense. In English the infinitive is the 'to' form of the verb, for example, 'to go' or 'to sing'. In Spanish the infinitive is a single word that ends in -ar, -er or -ir, for example **hablar**, **comer** or **vivir**.

> ### need to know
>
> **The forms of regular verbs are entirely predictable. If you learn** hablar, **for instance, you will know how to form all regular** -ar **verbs. Similarly,** comer **gives you a model for all regular** -er **verbs, and** vivir **for all regular** -ir **verbs. As in English, some of the most important verbs are irregular: for example,** ser **and** estar **'to be,** ir **'to go',** tener **and** haber **'to have'.**

Probably because Spanish verbs vary their endings according to who is doing the action, pronouns **yo**, **tú**, **ellos**, **ellas** and so on are often dropped. They tend to be used mainly for emphasis or when the subject would otherwise be unclear.

Like English, Spanish has two present tenses, the simple present (**hablo**, **hablas**, etc, like English 'I speak') and the present continuous (**estoy hablando**, **estás hablando**, etc, like English 'I am speaking'). The present continuous tends to be used specifically for activities that are happening at this very moment, while the present simple is more general, or for habitual actions:

> **estoy limpiando la cocina** I'm cleaning the kitchen
> **limpio la cocina todos los días** I clean the kitchen every day.

There is also more than one past tense. There is the preterite, a bit like the simple past in English: **hablaron** 'they spoke'; **no comieron nada** 'they didn't eat anything'. There is also the perfect tense (formed from the present of **haber** and a past participle): **¿lo has hecho?** 'did you do it?', **todavía no hemos comido** 'we haven't eaten yet'. This tense is often used to talk about things that have just happened. There is also the imperfect, for actions that happened repeatedly, or continued over a period of time, or which were happening at the time something else happened **cuando vivíamos en España comíamos cada día en el Bar Texas** 'when we were living in Spain we would have lunch in Bar Texas every day'.

Another important verb form is the 'subjunctive', used particularly to express uncertainty, doubt, possibility, feeling or wanting, when the subject of the second part of the sentence is not the same as that of the first: **quiero que te vayas** 'I want you to go', **no creo que fuera ella** 'I don't think it was her'; **me alegro de que hayas venido** 'I'm glad you've come'.

The subjunctive is also used in all negative commands ('don't do that, don't let's talk') and for all commands except those in the **tú** and **vosotros** forms: **siga todo recto** 'go straight on' (**usted** form); **póngame una cerveza** 'get me a beer' (**usted** form); **¡cuídense!** 'look after yourselves!' (**ustedes** form). And here are some negative examples: **no se preocupe** 'don't worry' (**usted** form); **no compremos nada** 'let's not buy anything'; **¡no habléis!** 'don't talk!' (**vosotros** form). When it comes to the **tú** and **vosotros** forms for instructions to do something, you use the 'imperative': **¡habla!** speak! (**tú** form); **¡hablad!** speak! (**vosotros** form).

> **need to know**
>
> Don't forget to put the little word **a** before words referring to people (and pets), when they're the direct object of any verb other than **tener**: **mató a su marido** 'she killed her husband'; **no vi al ladrón** 'I didn't see the thief' – but **tengo dos hijos** 'I've got two children'. When followed by **el** meaning 'the' it changes to **al**. This is what's called 'personal a', not to be confused with the preposition **a** meaning 'to', as in **ir al médico**, 'to go to the doctor's'.

In this section you will find some typical regular verbs and a selection of important irregular verbs, as well as examples showing the main tenses in use.

hablar (-ar verb, to speak, to talk)

Present			
	yo	hablo *ab-lo*	I don't speak French
	tú	hablas *ab-lass*	no **hablo** francés
	él/ella/se/Vd.	habla *ab-la*	*no **ab**-lo fran-**thess***
	nosotros(as)	hablamos *ab-**la**-moss*	
	vosotros(as)	habláis *ab-**la**-eess*	
	ellos/ellas/Vds.	hablan *ab-lan*	

Preterite		
	hablé *ab-**lay***	nobody spoke
	hablaste *ab-**lass**-tay*	nadie **habló**
	habló *ab-**lo***	***nad**-yay ab-**lo***
	hablamos *ab-**la**-moss*	
	hablasteis *ab-**lass**-tay-eess*	
	hablaron *ab-**la**-ron*	

Imperfect		
	hablaba *ab-**la**-ba*	she was joking
	hablabas *ab-**la**-bass*	**hablaba** en broma
	hablaba *ab-**la**-ba*	*ab-**la**-ba en **bro**-ma*
	hablábamos *ab-**la**-ba-moss*	
	hablabais *ab-**la**-ba-eess*	
	hablaban *ab-**la**-ban*	

Future		
	hablaré *ab-la-**ray***	I'll talk to her this evening
	hablarás *ab-la-**rass***	esta tarde **hablaré** con ella
	hablará *ab-la-**ra***	***ess**-ta **tar**-day ab-la-**ray** kon e-ya*
	hablaremos *ab-la-**rem**-os*	
	hablaréis *ab-la-**ray**-eess*	
	hablarán *ab-la-**ran***	

Conditional		
	hablaría *ab-la-**ree**-a*	what would you talk about?
	hablarías *ab-la-**ree**-ass*	¿de qué **hablarías**?
	hablaría *ab-la-**ree**-a*	*day kay ab-lar-**ee**-ass?*
	hablaríamos *ab-la-**ree**-a-moss*	
	hablaríais *ab-la-**ree**-a-eess*	
	hablarían *ab-la-**ree**-an*	

Subjunctive		
	hable *ab-**lay***	don't talk so loud
	hables *ab-**les***	no **hables** tan alto
	hable *ab-**lay***	*no **ab**-less tan **alt**-o*
	hablemos *ab-**lay**-moss*	
	habléis *ab-**lay**-eess*	
	hablen *ab-**len***	

Imperative	habla/hablad *ab-la/ab-**lad***	I've spoken to my sister
Gerund	hablando *ab-**land**-o*	he **hablado** con mi hermana
Past participle	hablado *ab-**lad**-o*	*ay ab-**lad**-o kon mee er-**ma**-na*

comer (-er verb, to eat)

Present	yo	como **ko**-mo	he/she doesn't eat meat
	tú	comes **ko**-mess	no **come** carne
	él/ella/se/Vd.	come **ko**-may	no **ko**-may **kar**-nay
	nosotros(as)	comemos ko-**mem**-oss	
	vosotros(as)	coméis ko-**may**-eess	
	ellos/ellas/Vds.	comen **ko**-men	

Preterite		comí ko-**mee**	we had lunch in a restaurant
		comiste ko-**mees**-tay	**comimos** en un restaurante
		comió kom-**yo**	ko-**mee**-moss en oon res-taoo-**ran**-tay
		comimos ko-**mee**-moss	
		comisteis ko-**mees**-tay-ees	
		comieron kom-**yer**-on	

Imperfect		comía ko-**mee**-a	they always ate too much
		comías ko-**mee**-ass	siempre **comían** demasiado
		comía ko-**mee**-a	**syem**-pray ko-**mee**-an dem-ass-**yad**-o
		comíamos ko-**mee**-a-moss	
		comíais ko-**mee**-a-eess	
		comían ko-**mee**-an	

Future		comeré ko-mer-**ay**	I'll eat it
		comerás ko-mer-**ass**	me lo **comeré** yo
		comerá ko-mer-**a**	may lo ko-mer-**ay** yo
		comeremos ko-mer-**ay**-moss	
		comeréis ko-mer-**ay**-eess	
		comerán ko-mer-**an**	

Conditional		comería ko-mer-**ee**-a	without money, we wouldn't eat
		comerías ko-mer-**ee**-ass	sin dinero, no **comeríamos**
		comería ko-mer-**ee**-a	seen dee-**ner**-o, no ko-mer-**ee**-a-moss
		comeríamos ko-mer-**ee**-a-moss	
		comeríais ko-mer-**ee**-a-eess	
		comerían ko-mer-**ee**-an	

Subjunctive		coma **ko**-ma	don't eat so fast
		comas **ko**-mass	no **comas** tan deprisa
		coma **ko**-ma	no **ko**-mass tan day-**pree**-sa
		comamos ko-**ma**-moss	
		comáis ko-**ma**-eess	
		coman **ko**-man	

Imperative		come/comed **ko**-may/ko-**med**	I haven't eaten today
Gerund		comiendo kom-**yend**-o	no he **comido** hoy
Past participle		comido ko-**meed**-o	no ay ko-**meed**-o oy

vivir (-ir verb, to live)

Present

yo	**vivo** *bee-bo*		where do you live?
tú	**vives** *bee-bess*		¿dónde **vives**?
él/ella/se/Vd.	**vive** *bee-bay*		*don-day bee-bess?*
nosotros(as)	**vivimos** *bee-bee-moss*		
vosotros(as)	**vivís** *bee-beess*		
ellos/ellas/Vds.	**viven** *bee-ben*		

Preterite

viví *bee-bee*
viviste *bee-bee-stay*
vivió *beeb-yo*
vivimos *bee-bee-moss*
vivisteis *bee-bee-stay-eess*
vivieron *beeb-yer-on*

he lived in the 13th century
vivió en el siglo XIII
beeb-yo en el seeg-lo treth-ay

Imperfect

vivía *bee-bee-a*
vivías *bee-bee-ass*
vivía *bee-bee-a*
vivíamos *bee-bee-a-moss*
vivíais *bee-bee-a-eess*
vivían *bee-bee-an*

they lived on his pension
vivían de su pensión
bee-bee-an day soo penss-yon

Future

viviré *bee-bee-ray*
vivirás *bee-bee-rass*
vivirá *bee-bee-ra*
viviremos *bee-beer-em-oss*
viviréis *bee-bee-ray-eess*
vivirán *bee-bee-ran*

we'll live in the city centre
viviremos en el centro de la ciudad
*bee-bee-ray-moss en el then-tro day
  la thyoo-dad*

Conditional

viviría *bee-bee-ree-a*
vivirías *bee-bee-ree-as*
viviría *bee-bee-ree-a*
viviríamos *bee-bee-ree-a-moss*
viviríais *bee-bee-ree-a-eess*
vivirían *bee-bee-ree-an*

we'd live in the country if we could
si pudiéramos, **viviríamos** en el campo
*see poo-dee-er-a-moss, bee-bee-ree-a-moss
  en el kam-po*

Subjunctive

viva *beeb-a*
vivas *beeb-ass*
viva *beeb-a*
vivamos *bee-ba-moss*
viváis *bee-ba-eess*
vivan *beeb-an*

long live the king!
¡**viva** el rey!
bee-ba el ray-ee!

Imperative **vive/vivid** *bee-bay/bee-beed*
Gerund **viviendo** *beeb-yend-o*
Past participle **vivido** *bee-beed-o*

they've always had a very comfortable life
siempre han **vivido** muy bien
syem-pray an bee-beed-o mwee byen

ser (to be)

Present			
yo	**soy** *soy*		I'm Spanish
tú	**eres** *er-ess*		**soy** español
él/ella/se/Vd.	**es** *ess*		*soy ess-pan-***yol**
nosotros(as)	**somos** *so-moss*		
vosotros(as)	**sois** *soyss*		
ellos/ellas/Vds.	**son** *son*		

Preterite		
fui *fwee*		was it you who phoned?
fuiste *fwee-stay*		¿**fuiste** tú el que llamó?
fue *fway*		**fwee-**stay too el kay ya-**mo?**
fuimos *fwee-moss*		
fuisteis *fwee-stay-eess*		
fueron *fwer-on*		

Imperfect		
era *er-a*		it was dark
eras *er-ass*		**era** de noche
era *er-a*		**er-**a day **notch-**ay
éramos *er-a-moss*		
erais *er-a-eess*		
eran *er-an*		

Future		
seré *ser-***ay**		it must be Joaquin's
serás *ser-***ass**		**será** de Joaquín
será *ser-a*		*ser-***a** day kho-a-**keen**
seremos *ser-***em-**oss*		
seréis *ser-***ay-**eess*		
serán *ser-***an**		

Conditional		
sería *ser-***ee-**a*		that would be great
serías *ser-***ee-**ass*		eso **sería** estupendo
sería *ser ***ec-**a*		**ess-**o se-**ree-**a ess-too-**pend-**o
seríamos *ser-***ee-**a-moss*		
seríais *ser-***ee-**a-eess*		
serían *ser-***ee-**an*		

Subjunctive		
sea *say-a*		don't be such a perfectionist!
seas *say-ass*		ino **seas** tan perfeccionista!
sea *say-a*		no **say-**ass tan perf-ekth-yon-**ee-**sta!
seamos *say-a-moss*		
seáis *say-***a-**eess*		
sean *say-an*		

Imperative	**sé/sed** *say/sed*		you've been very patient with him
Gerund	**siendo** *syend-o*		has **sido** muy paciente con él
Past participle	**sido** *seed-o*		ass **seed-**o mwee path-**yen-**tay kon el

estar (to be)

Present			
	yo	**estoy** ess-**toy**	I'm tired
	tú	**estás** ess-**tass**	**estoy** cansado
	él/ella/se/Vd.	**está** ess-**ta**	ess-**toy** kan-**sad**-o
	nosotros(as)	**estamos** ess-**tam**-oss	
	vosotros(as)	**estáis** ess-**tay**-eess	
	ellos/ellas/Vds.	**están** ess-**tan**	

Preterite		
	estuve ess-**too**-bay	we were at my parents' house
	estuviste ess-too-**bee**-stay	**estuvimos** en casa de mis padres
	estuvo ess-**too**-bo	ess-too-**bee**-moss en **ka**-sa day meess
	estuvimos ess-too-**bee**-moss	**pad**-ress
	estuvisteis ess-too-**bee**-stay-eess	
	estuvieron ess-toob-**yer**-on	

Imperfect		
	estaba ess-**tab**-a	where were you?
	estabas ess-**tab**-ass	¿dónde **estabas**?
	estaba ess-**tab**-a	**don**-day ess-**ta**-bass?
	estábamos ess-**tab**-a-moss	
	estabais ess-**tab**-a-eess	
	estaban ess-**tab**-an	

Future		
	estaré ess-ta-**ray**	what time will you be home?
	estarás ess-ta-**rass**	¿a qué hora **estarás** en casa?
	estará ess-ta-**ra**	a kay **o**-ra est-a-**ras** en **ka**-sa?
	estaremos ess-ta-**ray**-moss	
	estaréis ess-ta-**ray**-eess	
	estarán ess-ta-**ran**	

Conditional		
	estaría ess-ta-**ree**-a	she said she'd be here at eight o'clock
	estarías ess-ta-**ree**-ass	dijo que **estaría** aquí a las ocho
	estaría ess-ta-**ree**-a	**dee**-kho kay ess-ta-**ree**-a a los **otch**-o
	estaríamos ess-ta-**ree**-a-moss	
	estaríais ess-ta-**ree**-a-eess	
	estarían ess-ta-**ree**-an	

Subjunctive		
	esté ess-**tay**	let me know when you're ready
	estés esst-**tess**	avísame cuando **estés** lista
	esté ess-**tay**	a-**bee**-sa-may **kwand**-o es-**tayss** lee-sta
	estemos ess-**tay**-moss	
	estéis ess-**tay**-eess	
	estén ess-**ten**	

Imperative	**está/estad** ess-**ta**/ess-**tad**	have you ever been in Zaragoza?
Gerund	**estando** ess-**tand**-o	has **estado** alguna vez en Zaragoza?
Past participle	**estado** ess-**tad**-o	ass ess-**tad**-o al-**goo**-na beth en
		tha-ra-**goth**-a?

dar (to give)

Present	yo	**doy** *doy*	I'm afraid of the dark
	tú	**das** *dass*	me **da** miedo la oscuridad
	él/ella/se/Vd.	**da** *da*	*may da **myed**-o la os-koo-ree-**dad***
	nosotros(as)	**damos** *da-mos*	
	vosotros(as)	**dais** *da-eess*	
	ellos/ellas/Vds.	**dan** *dan*	

Preterite		**di** *dee*	they gave us a couple of free tickets
		diste *dee-stay*	nos **dieron** un par de entradas gratis
		dio *dyo*	*noss **dyer**-on oon par day ent-**ra**-dass*
		dimos *dee-moss*	***grat**-eess*
		disteis *dee-stay-eess*	
		dieron *dyer-on*	

Imperfect		**daba** *da-ba*	my window looked out onto the garden
		dabas *da-bass*	mi ventana **daba** al jardín
		daba *da-ba*	*mee ben-**ta**-na **da**-ba al khar-**deen***
		dábamos *da-ba-moss*	
		dabais *da-ba-eess*	
		daban *da-ban*	

Future		**daré** *da-ray*	I'll give you my mobile number
		darás *da-ras*	te **daré** el número de mi móvil
		dará *da-ra*	*tay da-**ray** el **noo-mer**-o day mee **mob**-eel*
		daremos *da-ray-moss*	
		daréis *da-ray-eess*	
		darán *da-ran*	

Conditional		**daría** *da-ree-a*	it would be lovely to see her again
		darías *da-ree-as*	me **daría** mucha alegría volver a verla
		daría *da-ree-a*	*may da-**ree**-a **mootch**-a a-leg-**ree**-a*
		daríamos *da-ree-a-moss*	*bol-**ver** a **ver**-la*
		daríais *da-ree-a-ess*	
		darían *dar-ee-an*	

Subjunctive		**dé** *day*	give me 2 kilos please
		des *dess*	**déme** dos kilos
		dé *day*	***dem**-ay doss **kee**-loss*
		demos *day-moss*	
		deis *day-eess*	
		den *den*	

Imperative		**da/dad** *da/dad*	his film's won several prizes
Gerund		**dando** *dand-o*	le han **dado** varios premios a su película
Past participle		**dado** *dad-o*	*lay han **dad**-o ba-ree-oss **prem**-yoss a soo*
			*pel-**ee**-koo-la*

tener (to have)

Present	yo	tengo **ten**-go	I'm thirsty
	tú	tienes **tyen**-ess	**tengo** sed
	él/ella/se/Vd.	tiene **tyen**-ay	**ten**-go sed
	nosotros(as)	tenemos te-**nem**-oss	
	vosotros(as)	tenéis ten-**ay**-eess	
	ellos/ellas/Vds.	tienen **tyen**-en	

Preterite		
	tuve **too**-bay	we had to leave
	tuviste too-**beest**-ay-eess	**tuvimos** que irnos
	tuvo **too**-bo	too-**bee**-moss kay **eer**-noss
	tuvimos too-**bee**-moss	
	tuvisteis too-**beest**-ay-eess	
	tuvieron toob-**yer**-on	

Imperfect		
	tenía ten-**ee**-ya	we didn't have enough money
	tenías ten-**ee**-ass	no **teníamos** suficiente dinero
	tenía ten-**ee**-a	no ten-**ee**-a-moss soo-feeth-**yen**-tay
	teníamos ten-**ee**-a-moss	dee-**ner**-o
	teníais ten-**ee**-a-eess	
	tenían ten-**ee**-an	

Future		
	tendré ten-**dray**	you'll have to pay for it yourself
	tendrás ten-**drass**	**tendrás** que pagarlo tú
	tendrá ten-**dra**	ten-**drass** kay pa-**gar**-lo too
	tendremos ten-**dray**-moss	
	tendréis ten-**dray**-eess	
	tendrán ten-**dran**	

Conditional		
	tendría ten-**dree**-a	you should eat more
	tendrías ten-**dree**-ass	**tendrías** que comer más
	tendría ten-**dree**-a	ten-**dree**-ass kay ko-**mer**-mass
	tendríamos ten-**dree**-a-moss	
	tendríais ten-**dree**-a-eess	
	tendrían ten-**dree**-an	

Subjunctive		
	tenga **ten**-ga	don't be afraid
	tengas **ten**-gass	no **tengas** miedo
	tenga **ten**-ga	no **ten**-gass **myed**-o
	tengamos ten-**ga**-moss	
	tengáis ten-**ga**-eess	
	tengan **ten**-gan	

Imperative	ten/tened ten/ten-**ed**	I've had a lot of problems
Gerund	teniendo ten-**yend**-o	he **tenido** muchos problemas
Past participle	tenido ten-**eed**-o	ay ten-**eed**-o **mootch**-oss prob-**lem**-ass

hacer (to do or make)

Present	yo	hago *ag-o*	what does your father do?
	tú	haces *ath-ess*	¿qué **hace** tu padre?
	él/ella/se/Vd.	hace *ath-ay*	*kay ath-ay too pad-ray?*
	nosotros(as)	hacemos *ath-ay-moss*	
	vosotros(as)	hacéis *ath-ay-eess*	
	ellos/ellas/Vds.	hacen *ath-en*	
Preterite		hice *eeth-ay*	they had the front of the school painted
		hiciste *eeth-ee-stay*	**hicieron** pintar la fachada del colegio
		hizo *eeth-o*	*eeth-yer-on peen-tar la fa-tcha-da del*
		hicimos *eeth-ee-moss*	*ko-lekh-yo*
		hiciste *eeth-ee-stay-eess*	
		hicieron *eeth-yer-on*	
Imperfect		hacía *ath-ee-ya*	he did it to annoy me
		hacías *ath-ee-ass*	lo **hacía** para fastidiarme
		hacía *ath-ee-a*	*lo ath-ee-ya pa-ra fas-tee-dee-ar-may*
		hacíamos *ath-ee-a-moss*	
		hacíais *ath-ee-a-eess*	
		hacían *ath-ee-an*	
Future		haré *a-ray*	I'll do it myself
		harás *a-rass*	lo **haré** yo mismo
		hará *a-ra*	*lo a-ray yo mees-mo*
		haremos *a-ray-moss*	
		haréis *a-ray-eess*	
		harán *a-ran*	
Conditional		haría *a-ree-a*	you said you'd do it
		harías *a-ree-ass*	dijiste que lo **harías**
		haría *a-ree-a*	*dee-khee-stay kay lo ar-ee-ass*
		haríamos *a-ree-a-moss*	
		haríais *a-ree-a-eess*	
		harían *a-ree-an*	
Subjunctive		haga *a-ga*	do you want me to make the beds?
		hagas *a-gass*	¿quieres que **haga** las camas?
		haga *a-ga*	*kyer-ess kay a-ga lass ka-mass?*
		hagamos *a-ga-moss*	
		hagáis *a-ga-eess*	
		hagan *a-gan*	
Imperative		haz/haced *ath/ath-ed*	who did that?
Gerund		haciendo *ath-yend-o*	¿quién ha **hecho** eso?
Past participle		hecho *etch-o*	*kyen a etch-o ess-o?*

ir (to go)

Present

yo	**voy** *boy*	where are you going?
tú	**vas** *bass*	¿dónde **vas**?
él/ella/se/Vd.	**va** *ba*	**don**-day bass?
nosotros(as)	**vamos** **ba**-*moss*	
vosotros(as)	**vais** **ba**-*eess*	
ellos/ellas/Vds.	**van** **ban**	

Preterite

fui *fwee*	we went to the cinema last night
fuiste **fwee**-*stay*	anoche **fuimos** al cine
fue *fway*	an-**otch**-ay **fwee**-moss al **thee**-nay
fuimos **fwee**-*moss*	
fuisteis **fwee**-*stay-eess*	
fueron **fwer**-*on*	

Imperfect

iba **eeb**-*a*	he was very well dressed
ibas **eeb**-*ass*	**iba** muy bien vestido
iba **eeb**-*a*	**ee**-ba mwee byen bess-**teed**-o
íbamos **eeb**-*a-moss*	
ibais **eeb**-*a-eess*	
iban **eeb**-*an*	

Future

iré *ee-**ray***	I'm going to Edinburgh on Sunday
irás *ee-**rass***	el domingo **iré** a Edimburgo
irá *ee-**ra***	el do-**meen**-go ee-**ray** a ed-een-**boor**-go
iremos *ee-**ray**-moss*	
iréis *ee-**ray**-eess*	
irán *ee-**ran***	

Conditional

iría *ee-**ree**-a*	they said they'd walk
irías *ee-**ree**-a-eess*	dijeron que **irían** andando
iría *ee-**ree**-a*	dee-**kher**-on kay ee-**ree**-an an-**dand**-o
iríamos *ee-**ree**-a-moss*	
iríais *ee-**ree**-a-eess*	
irían *ee-**ree**-an*	

Subjunctive

vaya **ba**-*ya*	don't leave without saying goodbye
vayas **ba**-*yass*	no te **vayas** sin despedirte
vaya **ba**-*ya*	no tay **ba**-yass seen dess-ped-**eer**-tay
vayamos **ba**-*ya-moss*	
vayáis **ba**-*ya-eess*	
vayan **ba**-*yan*	

Imperative   **ve/id** *bay/eed*   she has gone to buy the bread
Gerund   **yendo** **yend**-*o*   ha **ido** a comprar el pan
Past participle   **ido** **eed**-*o*   a **eed**-o a komp-**rar** el pan

haber (to have – auxiliary verb)

Present	yo	**he** *hay*	did you see that?
	tú	**has** *ass*	¿**has** visto eso?
	él/ella/se/Vd.	**ha** *a*	as **bee**-sto **ess**-o?
	nosotros(as)	**hemos** *ay-moss*	
	vosotros(as)	**habéis** *a-bay-eess*	
	ellos/ellas/Vds.	**han** *an*	

Preterite		**hube** *oo-bay*	there were a lot of problems
		hubiste *oo-bee-stay*	**hubo** muchos problemas
		hubo *oo-bo*	**oo**-bo **mootch**-oss prob-**lem**-ass
		hubimos *oo-bee-moss*	
		hubisteis *oo-bee-stay-eess*	
		hubieron *oob-yer-on*	

Imperfect		**había** *a-bee-a*	there was always too much work
		habías *a-bee-ass*	siempre **había** demasiado trabajo
		había *a-bee-a*	**syem**-pray a-**bee**-a dem-ass-**yad**-o
		habíamos *a-bee-a-moss*	trab-**a**-kho
		habíais *a-bee-a-eess*	
		habían *a-bee-an*	

Future		**habré** *ab-ray*	it will have to be cleaned
		habrás *ab-rass*	**habrá** que limpiarlo
		habrá *ab-ra*	ab-**ra** kay leemp-**yar**-lo
		habremos *ab-ray-moss*	
		habréis *ab-ray-eess*	
		habrán *ab-ran*	

Conditional		**habría** *ab-ree-a*	it ought to be cleaned
		habrías *ab-ree-ass*	**habría** que limpiarlo
		habría *ab-ree-a*	ab-**ree**-a kay leemp-**yar**-lo
		habríamos *ab-ree-a-moss*	
		habríais *ab-ree-a-eess*	
		habrían *ab-ree-an*	

Subjunctive		**haya** *a-ya*	I don't think there'll be any problem
		hayas *a-yan*	no creo que **haya** ningún problema
		haya *a-ya*	no **kray**-o kay *a*-ya neen-**goon** prob-**lem**-a
		hayamos *a-ya-moss*	
		hayáis *a-ya-eess*	
		hayan *a-yan*	

Imperative		(not used)	there has been an earthquake in Iran
Gerund		**habiendo** *ab-yend-o*	ha **habido** un terremoto en Irán
Past participle		**habido** *a-beed-o*	a a-**beed**-o oon ter-rem-**ot**-o en ee-**ran**

poder (to be able to)

Present			
	yo	**puedo** *pwed-o*	can I come in?
	tú	**puedes** *pwed-ess*	¿**puedo** entrar?
	él/ella/se/Vd.	**puede** *pwed-ay*	*pwed-o en-**trar**?*
	nosotros(as)	**podemos** *pod-**ay**-moss*	
	vosotros(as)	**podéis** *pod-**ay**-eess*	
	ellos/ellas/Vds.	**pueden** *pwed-en*	

Preterite		
pude *pood-ay*	you could have hurt yourself
pudiste *pood-**ees**-tay*	**pudiste** haberte hecho daño
pudo *pood-o*	*pood-**ee**-stay a-**ber**-tay **etch**-o **dan**-yo*
pudimos *pood-**ee**-moss*	
pudisteis *pood-**ee**-stay-eess*	
pudieron *pood-**yer**-on*	

Imperfect		
podía *pod-**ee**-a*	you could have told me!
podías *pod-**ee**-ass*	ime lo **podías** haber dicho!
podía *pod-**ee**-a*	*may lo pod-**ee**-as a-**ber deetch**-o!*
podíamos *pod-**ee**-a-moss*	
podíais *pod-**ee**-a-eess*	
podían *pod-**ee**-an*	

Future		
podré *pod-**ray***	I'm sure he'll succeed
podrás *pod-**rass***	estoy segura de que **podrá** conseguirlo
podrá *pod-**ra***	*ess-**toy** se-**goo**-ra day kay pod-**ra***
podremos *pod-**ray**-moss*	*kon-seg-**eer**-lo*
podréis *pod-**ray**-eess*	
podrán *pod-**ran***	

Conditional		
podría *pod-**ree**-a*	could you help me?
podrías *pod-**ree**-as*	¿**podrías** ayudarme?
podría *pod-**ree**-a*	*pod-**ree**-ass a-yoo-**dar**-may?*
podríamos *pod-**ree**-a-moss*	
podríais *pod-**ree**-a-eess*	
podrían *pod-**ree**-an*	

Subjunctive		
pueda *pwed-a*	come as soon as you can
puedas *pwed-ass*	ven en cuanto **puedas**
pueda *pwed-a*	*ben en **kwan**-to **pwed**-ass*
podamos *pod-**a**-moss*	
podáis *pod-**a**-eess*	
puedan *pwed-an*	

Imperative	**puede/poded** *pwed-ay/pod-ed*	I couldn't come before
Gerund	**pudiendo** *pood-**yend**-o*	no he **podido** venir antes
Past participle	**podido** *pod-**eed**-o*	*no ay pod-**eed**-o ben-**eer** an-tess*

querer (to want, to love)

Present	yo	**quiero** *kyer-o*	I love you
	tú	**quieres** *kyer-ess*	te **quiero**
	él/ella/se/Vd.	**quiere** *kyer-ay*	tay **kyer**-o
	nosotros(as)	**queremos** *ke-rem-oss*	
	vosotros(as)	**queréis** *ke-ray-eess*	
	ellos/ellas/Vds.	**quieren** *kyer-en*	

Preterite	**quise** *kee-say*	he wanted to do it but he couldn't
	quisiste *kee-seess-tay*	**quiso** hacerlo pero no pudo
	quiso *kee-so*	**kee**-so ath-**er**-lo pe-ro no **pood**-o
	quisimos *kee-see-moss*	
	quisisteis *kee-seess-tay-eess*	
	quisieron *keess-yer-on*	

Imperfect	**quería** *ker-ee-a*	she didn't want to tell me
	querías *ker-ee-as*	no **quería** decírmelo
	quería *ker-ee-a*	no ker-**ee**-a deth-eer-**mel**-o
	queríamos *ker-ee-a-mos*	
	queríais *ker-ee-a-eess*	
	querían *ker-ee-an*	

Future	**querré** *ker-ray*	will you sign me your autograph?
	querrás *ker-rass*	¿**querrá** firmarme un autógrafo?
	querrá *ker-ra*	ker-**ra** feer-**mar**-may oon aoo-**tog**-ra-fo?
	querremos *ker-ray-moss*	
	querréis *ker-ray-eess*	
	querrán *ker-ran*	

Conditional	**querría** *ker-ree-a*	I wish it had never happened
	querrías *ker-ree-as*	**querría** que no hubiera pasado nunca
	querría *ker-ree-a*	ker-**ree**-a kay no oob-**yer**-a pa-**sad**-o
	querríamos *ker-ree-a-mos*	**noon**-ka
	querríais *ker-ree-a-eess*	
	querrían *ker-ree-an*	

Subjunctive	**quiera** *kyer-a*	whether you like it or not, it's going to
	quieras *kyer-ass*	change our lives
	quiera *kyer-a*	**quieras** o no, eso cambiará nuestras
	queramos *ker-a-moss*	vidas
	queráis *ker-a-eess*	ker-**ee**-ass o no, **ess**-o kamb-**ya**-ra
	quieran *kyer-an*	**nwess**-trass **bee**-dass

Imperative	**quiere/quered** *kyer-ay/ker-ed*	you really asked for it!
Gerund	**queriendo** *ker-yend-o*	¡es que tú lo has **querido**!
Past participle	**querido** *ke-reed-o*	ess kay too lo as ke-**reed**-o!

saber (to know)

Present			
yo	**sé** *say*	I don't know
tú	**sabes** *sa-bess*	no lo **sé**
él/ella/se/Vd.	**sabe** *sa-bay*	*no lo say*
nosotros(as)	**sabemos** *sa-**bay**-moss*	
vosotros(as)	**sabéis** *sa-**bay**-eess*	
ellos/ellas/Vds.	**saben** *sa-ben*	

Preterite
supe *soo-pay* — I didn't know what to answer
supiste *soo-**pee**-stay* — no **supe** qué responder
supo *soo-po* — *no **soo**-pay kay ress-pon-**der***
supimos *soo-**pee**-moss*
supisteis *soo-**pee**-stay-eess*
supieron *soo-**pyer**-on*

Imperfect
sabía *sa-**bee**-a* — I thought you knew
sabías *sa-**bee**-ass* — pensaba que lo **sabías**
sabía *sa-**bee**-a* — *pen-**sa**-ba kay lo sa-**bee**-ass*
sabíamos *sab-**ee**-a-moss*
sabíais *sa-**bee**-a-eess*
sabían *sa-**bee**-an*

Future
sabré *sab-**ray*** — we will never know who killed her
sabrás *sab-**rass*** — nunca se **sabrá** quién la mató
sabrá *sab-**ra*** — ***noon**-ka say sab-**ra** kyen la ma-**to***
sabremos *sab-**rem**-oss*
sabréis *sab-**re**-eess*
sabrán *sab-**ran***

Conditional
sabría *sab-**ree**-a* — if you weren't so afraid, you'd be able to swim already
sabrías *sab-**ree**-ass* — si no tuvieras tanto miedo, ya **sabrías** nadar
sabría *sab-**ree**-a* — *see no toob-**yer**-as **tan**-to **myed**-o,*
sabríamos *sab-**ree**-a-moss* — *ya sab-**ree**-ass na-**dar***
sabríais *sab-**ree**-a-eess*
sabrían *sab-**ree**-an*

Subjunctive
sepa *sep-a* — as far as I know
sepas *sep-as* — que yo **sepa**
sepa *sep-a* — *kay yo **sep**-a*
sepamos *sep-**a**-moss*
sepáis *sep-**a**-eess*
sepan *sep-an*

Imperative — **sabe/sabed** *sa-bay/sa-**bed*** — when did you find out?
Gerund — **sabiendo** *sab-**yen**-do* — ¿cuándo lo has **sabido?**
Past participle — **sabido** *sab-**ee**-do* — ***kwan**-do ass sa-**bee**-do?*